Coriolanus by William Shakespeare

The life of William Shakespeare, arguably the most significant figure in the Western literary canon, is relatively unknown.

Shakespeare was born in Stratford-upon-Avon in 1565, possibly on the 23rd April, St. George's Day, and baptised there on 26th April.

Little is known of his education and the first firm facts to his life relate to his marriage, aged 18, to Anne Hathaway, who was 26 and from the nearby village of Shottery. Anne gave birth to their first son six months later.

Shakespeare's first play, The Comedy of Errors began a procession of real heavyweights that were to emanate from his pen in a career of just over twenty years in which 37 plays were written and his reputation forever established.

This early skill was recognised by many and by 1594 the Lord Chamberlain's Men were performing his works. With the advantage of Shakespeare's progressive writing they rapidly became London's leading company of players, affording him more exposure and, following the death of Queen Elizabeth in 1603, a royal patent by the new king, James I, at which point they changed their name to the King's Men.

By 1598, and despite efforts to pirate his work, Shakespeare's name was well known and had become a selling point in its own right on title pages.

No plays are attributed to Shakespeare after 1613, and the last few plays he wrote before this time were in collaboration with other writers, one of whom is likely to be John Fletcher who succeeded him as the house playwright for the King's Men.

William Shakespeare died two months later on April 23rd, 1616, survived by his wife, two daughters and a legacy of writing that none have since yet eclipsed.

Index of Contents
DRAMATIS PERSONAE
ACT I
Scene I - Rome. A Street.
Scene II - Corioli. The Senate House.
Scene III - Rome. A Room in Marcius' House.
Scene IV - Before Corioli.
Scene V - Corioli. A Street.
Scene VI - Near the Camp of Cominius.
Scene VII - The Gates of Corioli.
Scene VIII - A Field of Battle.
Scene IX - The Roman Camp.
Scene X - The Camp of the Volsces.
ACT II

Scene I - Rome. A Public Place.
Scene II - The Same. The Capitol.
Scene III - The Same. The Forum.
ACT III
Scene I - Rome. A Street.
Scene II - A Room in Coriolanus's House.
Scene III - The Same. The Forum.
ACT IV
Scene I - Rome. Before a Gate of the City.
Scene II - The Same. A Street Near the Gate.
Scene III - A Highway Between Rome and Antium.
Scene IV - Antium. Before Aufidius's House.
Scene V - The Same. A Hall in Aufidius's House.
Scene VI - Rome. A Public Place.
Scene VII - A Camp, at a Small Distance from Rome.
ACT V
Scene I - Rome. A Public Place.
Scene II - Entrance of the Volscian Camp Before Rome.
Scene III - The Tent of Coriolanus.
Scene IV - Rome. A Public Place.
Scene V - The Same. A Street Near the Gate.
Scene VI - Antium. A Public Place.
William Shakespeare – A Short Biography
William Shakespeare – A Concise Bibliography
Shakespeare; or, the Poet by Ralph Waldo Emerson
William Shakespeare – A Tribute in Verse

DRAMATIS PERSONAE
CAIUS MARCIUS, afterwards Caius Marcius Coriolanus
VOLUMNIA, Mother to Coriolanus
VIRGILIA, Wife to Coriolanus
VALERIA, Friend to Virgilia
TITUS LARTIUS, & COMINIUS, Generals against the Volscians
MENENIUS AGRIPPA, Friend to Coriolanus
SICINIUS VELUTUS, & JUNIUS BRUTUS, Tribunes of the People
YOUNG MARCIUS, Son to Coriolanus
TULLUS AUFIDIUS, General of the Volscians
Lieutenant to Aufidius
Conspirators with Aufidius
NICANOR, a Roman
A Roman Herald
A Citizen of Antium
ADRIAN, a Volsce
Two Volscian Guards
Gentlewoman, attending on Virgilia
Roman and Volscian Senators, Patricians, Ædiles, Lictors, Soldiers, Citizens, Messengers, Servants to Aufidius, and other Attendants

SCENE—Rome and the Neighbourhood; Corioli and the Neighbourhood; Antium.

ACT I

SCENE I. Rome. A street.

Enter a company of mutinous CITIZENS, with staves, clubs, and other weapons

FIRST CITIZEN
Before we proceed any further, hear me speak.

ALL
Speak, speak.

FIRST CITIZEN
You are all resolved rather to die than to famish?

ALL
Resolved. resolved.

FIRST CITIZEN
First, you know Caius Marcius is chief enemy to the people.

ALL
We know't, we know't.

FIRST CITIZEN
Let us kill him, and we'll have corn at our own price.
Is't a verdict?

ALL
No more talking on't; let it be done: away, away!

SECOND CITIZEN
One word, good citizens.

FIRST CITIZEN
We are accounted poor citizens, the patricians good. What authority surfeits on would relieve us: if they would yield us but the superfluity, while it were wholesome, we might guess they relieved us humanely; but they think we are too dear: the leanness that afflicts us, the object of our misery, is as an inventory to particularise their abundance; our sufferance is a gain to them Let us revenge this with our pikes, ere we become rakes: for the gods know I speak this in hunger for bread, not in thirst for revenge.

SECOND CITIZEN
Would you proceed especially against Caius Marcius?

ALL

Against him first: he's a very dog to the commonalty.

SECOND CITIZEN
Consider you what services he has done for his country?

FIRST CITIZEN
Very well; and could be content to give him good report fort, but that he pays himself with being proud.

SECOND CITIZEN
Nay, but speak not maliciously.

FIRST CITIZEN
I say unto you, what he hath done famously, he did it to that end: though soft-conscienced men can be content to say it was for his country he did it to please his mother and to be partly proud; which he is, even till the altitude of his virtue.

SECOND CITIZEN
What he cannot help in his nature, you account a vice in him. You must in no way say he is covetous.

FIRST CITIZEN
If I must not, I need not be barren of accusations; he hath faults, with surplus, to tire in repetition.

Shouts within

What shouts are these? The other side o' the city is risen: why stay we prating here? to the Capitol!

ALL
Come, come.

FIRST CITIZEN
Soft! who comes here?

Enter MENENIUS AGRIPPA

SECOND CITIZEN
Worthy Menenius Agrippa; one that hath always loved the people.

FIRST CITIZEN
He's one honest enough: would all the rest were so!

MENENIUS
What work's, my countrymen, in hand? where go you
With bats and clubs? The matter? speak, I pray you.

FIRST CITIZEN
Our business is not unknown to the senate; they have had inkling this fortnight what we intend to do, which now we'll show 'em in deeds. They say poor suitors have strong breaths: they shall know we have strong arms too.

MENENIUS

Why, masters, my good friends, mine honest neighbours,
Will you undo yourselves?

FIRST CITIZEN
We cannot, sir, we are undone already.

MENENIUS
I tell you, friends, most charitable care
Have the patricians of you. For your wants,
Your suffering in this dearth, you may as well
Strike at the heaven with your staves as lift them
Against the Roman state, whose course will on
The way it takes, cracking ten thousand curbs
Of more strong link asunder than can ever
Appear in your impediment. For the dearth,
The gods, not the patricians, make it, and
Your knees to them, not arms, must help. Alack,
You are transported by calamity
Thither where more attends you, and you slander
The helms o' the state, who care for you like fathers,
When you curse them as enemies.

FIRST CITIZEN
Care for us! True, indeed! They ne'er cared for us yet: suffer us to famish, and their store-houses crammed with grain; make edicts for usury, to support usurers; repeal daily any wholesome act established against the rich, and provide more piercing statutes daily, to chain up and restrain the poor. If the wars eat us not up, they will; and there's all the love they bear us.

MENENIUS
Either you must
Confess yourselves wondrous malicious,
Or be accused of folly. I shall tell you
A pretty tale: it may be you have heard it;
But, since it serves my purpose, I will venture
To stale 't a little more.

FIRST CITIZEN
Well, I'll hear it, sir: yet you must not think to fob off our disgrace with a tale: but, an 't please you, deliver.

MENENIUS
There was a time when all the body's members
Rebell'd against the belly, thus accused it:
That only like a gulf it did remain
I' the midst o' the body, idle and unactive,
Still cupboarding the viand, never bearing
Like labour with the rest, where the other instruments
Did see and hear, devise, instruct, walk, feel,
And, mutually participate, did minister
Unto the appetite and affection common
Of the whole body. The belly answer'd—

FIRST CITIZEN
Well, sir, what answer made the belly?

MENENIUS
Sir, I shall tell you. With a kind of smile,
Which ne'er came from the lungs, but even thus—
For, look you, I may make the belly smile
As well as speak—it tauntingly replied
To the discontented members, the mutinous parts
That envied his receipt; even so most fitly
As you malign our senators for that
They are not such as you.

FIRST CITIZEN
Your belly's answer? What!
The kingly-crowned head, the vigilant eye,
The counsellor heart, the arm our soldier,
Our steed the leg, the tongue our trumpeter.
With other muniments and petty helps
In this our fabric, if that they—

MENENIUS
What then?
'Fore me, this fellow speaks! What then? what then?

FIRST CITIZEN
Should by the cormorant belly be restrain'd,
Who is the sink o' the body,—

MENENIUS
Well, what then?

FIRST CITIZEN
The former agents, if they did complain,
What could the belly answer?

MENENIUS
I will tell you
If you'll bestow a small—of what you have little
Patience awhile, you'll hear the belly's answer.

FIRST CITIZEN
Ye're long about it.

MENENIUS
Note me this, good friend;
Your most grave belly was deliberate,
Not rash like his accusers, and thus answer'd:
'True is it, my incorporate friends,' quoth he,
'That I receive the general food at first,

Which you do live upon; and fit it is,
Because I am the store-house and the shop
Of the whole body: but, if you do remember,
I send it through the rivers of your blood,
Even to the court, the heart, to the seat o' the brain;
And, through the cranks and offices of man,
The strongest nerves and small inferior veins
From me receive that natural competency
Whereby they live: and though that all at once,
You, my good friends,' this says the belly, mark me,

FIRST CITIZEN
Ay, sir; well, well.

MENENIUS
'Though all at once cannot
See what I do deliver out to each,
Yet I can make my audit up, that all
From me do back receive the flour of all,
And leave me but the bran.' What say you to't?

FIRST CITIZEN
It was an answer: how apply you this?

MENENIUS
The senators of Rome are this good belly,
And you the mutinous members; for examine
Their counsels and their cares, digest things rightly
Touching the weal o' the common, you shall find
No public benefit which you receive
But it proceeds or comes from them to you
And no way from yourselves. What do you think,
You, the great toe of this assembly?

FIRST CITIZEN
I the great toe! why the great toe?

MENENIUS
For that, being one o' the lowest, basest, poorest,
Of this most wise rebellion, thou go'st foremost:
Thou rascal, that art worst in blood to run,
Lead'st first to win some vantage.
But make you ready your stiff bats and clubs:
Rome and her rats are at the point of battle;
The one side must have bale.

Enter CAIUS MARCIUS

Hail, noble Marcius!

MARCIUS

Thanks. What's the matter, you dissentious rogues,
That, rubbing the poor itch of your opinion,
Make yourselves scabs?

FIRST CITIZEN
We have ever your good word.

MARCIUS
He that will give good words to thee will flatter
Beneath abhorring. What would you have, you curs,
That like nor peace nor war? the one affrights you,
The other makes you proud. He that trusts to you,
Where he should find you lions, finds you hares;
Where foxes, geese: you are no surer, no,
Than is the coal of fire upon the ice,
Or hailstone in the sun. Your virtue is
To make him worthy whose offence subdues him
And curse that justice did it.
Who deserves greatness
Deserves your hate; and your affections are
A sick man's appetite, who desires most that
Which would increase his evil. He that depends
Upon your favours swims with fins of lead
And hews down oaks with rushes. Hang ye! Trust Ye?
With every minute you do change a mind,
And call him noble that was now your hate,
Him vile that was your garland. What's the matter,
That in these several places of the city
You cry against the noble senate, who,
Under the gods, keep you in awe, which else
Would feed on one another? What's their seeking?

MENENIUS
For corn at their own rates; whereof, they say,
The city is well stored.

MARCIUS
Hang 'em! They say!
They'll sit by the fire, and presume to know
What's done i' the Capitol; who's like to rise,
Who thrives and who declines; side factions and give out
Conjectural marriages; making parties strong
And feebling such as stand not in their liking
Below their cobbled shoes. They say there's grain enough!
Would the nobility lay aside their ruth,
And let me use my sword, I'll make a quarry
With thousands of these quarter'd slaves, as high
As I could pick my lance.

MENENIUS

Nay, these are almost thoroughly persuaded;
For though abundantly they lack discretion,
Yet are they passing cowardly. But, I beseech you,
What says the other troop?

MARCIUS
They are dissolved: hang 'em!
They said they were an-hungry; sigh'd forth proverbs,
That hunger broke stone walls, that dogs must eat,
That meat was made for mouths, that the gods sent not
Corn for the rich men only: with these shreds
They vented their complainings; which being answer'd,
And a petition granted them, a strange one—
To break the heart of generosity,
And make bold power look pale—they threw their caps
As they would hang them on the horns o' the moon,
Shouting their emulation.

MENENIUS
What is granted them?

MARCIUS
Five tribunes to defend their vulgar wisdoms,
Of their own choice: one's Junius Brutus,
Sicinius Velutus, and I know not—'Sdeath!
The rabble should have first unroof'd the city,
Ere so prevail'd with me: it will in time
Win upon power and throw forth greater themes
For insurrection's arguing.

MENENIUS
This is strange.

MARCIUS
Go, get you home, you fragments!

Enter a MESSENGER, hastily

MESSENGER
Where's Caius Marcius?

MARCIUS
Here: what's the matter?

MESSENGER
The news is, sir, the Volsces are in arms.

MARCIUS
I am glad on 't: then we shall ha' means to vent
Our musty superfluity. See, our best elders.

Enter COMINIUS, TITUS LARTIUS, and other SENATORS; JUNIUS BRUTUS and SICINIUS VELUTUS

FIRST SENATOR
Marcius, 'tis true that you have lately told us;
The Volsces are in arms.

MARCIUS
They have a leader,
Tullus Aufidius, that will put you to 't.
I sin in envying his nobility,
And were I anything but what I am,
I would wish me only he.

COMINIUS
You have fought together.

MARCIUS
Were half to half the world by the ears and he.
Upon my party, I'ld revolt to make
Only my wars with him: he is a lion
That I am proud to hunt.

FIRST SENATOR
Then, worthy Marcius,
Attend upon Cominius to these wars.

COMINIUS
It is your former promise.

MARCIUS
Sir, it is;
And I am constant. Titus Lartius, thou
Shalt see me once more strike at Tullus' face.
What, art thou stiff? stand'st out?

TITUS
No, Caius Marcius;
I'll lean upon one crutch and fight with t'other,
Ere stay behind this business.

MENENIUS
O, true-bred!

FIRST SENATOR
Your company to the Capitol; where, I know,
Our greatest friends attend us.

TITUS
[To COMINIUS] Lead you on.
To MARCIUS
Right worthy you priority.

COMINIUS
Noble Marcius!

FIRST SENATOR
[To the Citizens] Hence to your homes; be gone!

MARCIUS
Nay, let them follow:
The Volsces have much corn; take these rats thither
To gnaw their garners. Worshipful mutiners,
Your valour puts well forth: pray, follow.

CITIZENS steal away.

Exeunt all but SICINIUS and BRUTUS

SICINIUS
Was ever man so proud as is this Marcius?

BRUTUS
He has no equal.

SICINIUS
When we were chosen tribunes for the people,—

BRUTUS
Mark'd you his lip and eyes?

SICINIUS
Nay. but his taunts.

BRUTUS
Being moved, he will not spare to gird the gods.

SICINIUS
Be-mock the modest moon.

BRUTUS
The present wars devour him: he is grown
Too proud to be so valiant.

SICINIUS
Such a nature,
Tickled with good success, disdains the shadow
Which he treads on at noon: but I do wonder
His insolence can brook to be commanded
Under Cominius.

BRUTUS

Fame, at the which he aims,
In whom already he's well graced, can not
Better be held nor more attain'd than by
A place below the first: for what miscarries
Shall be the general's fault, though he perform
To the utmost of a man, and giddy censure
Will then cry out of Marcius 'O if he
Had borne the business!'

SICINIUS
Besides, if things go well,
Opinion that so sticks on Marcius shall
Of his demerits rob Cominius.

BRUTUS
Come:
Half all Cominius' honours are to Marcius.
Though Marcius earned them not, and all his faults
To Marcius shall be honours, though indeed
In aught he merit not.

SICINIUS
Let's hence, and hear
How the dispatch is made, and in what fashion,
More than his singularity, he goes
Upon this present action.

BRUTUS
Lets along.

Exeunt

SCENE II. Corioli. The Senate House.

Enter TULLUS AUFIDIUS and certain SENATORS

FIRST SENATOR
So, your opinion is, Aufidius,
That they of Rome are entered in our counsels
And know how we proceed.

AUFIDIUS
Is it not yours?
What ever have been thought on in this state,
That could be brought to bodily act ere Rome
Had circumvention? 'Tis not four days gone
Since I heard thence; these are the words: I think
I have the letter here; yes, here it is.

Reads
'They have press'd a power, but it is not known
Whether for east or west: the dearth is great;
The people mutinous; and it is rumour'd,
Cominius, Marcius your old enemy,
Who is of Rome worse hated than of you,
And Titus Lartius, a most valiant Roman,
These three lead on this preparation
Whither 'tis bent: most likely 'tis for you:
Consider of it.'

FIRST SENATOR
Our army's in the field
We never yet made doubt but Rome was ready
To answer us.

AUFIDIUS
Nor did you think it folly
To keep your great pretences veil'd till when
They needs must show themselves; which
in the hatching,
It seem'd, appear'd to Rome. By the discovery.
We shall be shorten'd in our aim, which was
To take in many towns ere almost Rome
Should know we were afoot.

SECOND SENATOR
Noble Aufidius,
Take your commission; hie you to your bands:
Let us alone to guard Corioli:
If they set down before 's, for the remove
Bring your army; but, I think, you'll find
They've not prepared for us.

AUFIDIUS
O, doubt not that;
I speak from certainties. Nay, more,
Some parcels of their power are forth already,
And only hitherward. I leave your honours.
If we and Caius Marcius chance to meet,
'Tis sworn between us we shall ever strike
Till one can do no more.

ALL
The gods assist you!

AUFIDIUS
And keep your honours safe!

FIRST SENATOR
Farewell.

SECOND SENATOR
Farewell.

ALL
Farewell.

Exeunt

SCENE III. Rome. A Room in Marcius' House.

Enter VOLUMNIA and VIRGILIA they set them down on two low stools, and sew

VOLUMNIA
I pray you, daughter, sing; or express yourself in a more comfortable sort: if my son were my husband, I should freelier rejoice in that absence wherein he won honour than in the embracements of his bed where he would show most love. When yet he was but tender-bodied and the only son of my womb, when youth with comeliness plucked all gaze his way, when for a day of kings' entreaties a mother should not sell him an hour from her beholding, I, considering how honour would become such a person. that it was no better than picture-like to hang by the wall, if renown made it not stir, was pleased to let him seek danger where he was like to find fame. To a cruel war I sent him; from whence he returned, his brows bound with oak. I tell thee, daughter, I sprang not more in joy at first hearing he was a man-child than now in first seeing he had proved himself a man.

VIRGILIA
But had he died in the business, madam; how then?

VOLUMNIA
Then his good report should have been my son; I therein would have found issue. Hear me profess sincerely: had I a dozen sons, each in my love alike and none less dear than thine and my good Marcius, I had rather had eleven die nobly for their country than one voluptuously surfeit out of action.

Enter a GENTLEWOMAN

GENTLEWOMAN
Madam, the Lady Valeria is come to visit you.

VIRGILIA
Beseech you, give me leave to retire myself.

VOLUMNIA
Indeed, you shall not.
Methinks I hear hither your husband's drum,
See him pluck Aufidius down by the hair,
As children from a bear, the Volsces shunning him:
Methinks I see him stamp thus, and call thus:
'Come on, you cowards! you were got in fear,
Though you were born in Rome:' his bloody brow

With his mail'd hand then wiping, forth he goes,
Like to a harvest-man that's task'd to mow
Or all or lose his hire.

VIRGILIA
His bloody brow! O Jupiter, no blood!

VOLUMNIA
Away, you fool! it more becomes a man
Than gilt his trophy: the breasts of Hecuba,
When she did suckle Hector, look'd not lovelier
Than Hector's forehead when it spit forth blood
At Grecian sword, contemning. Tell Valeria,
We are fit to bid her welcome.

Exit GENTLEWOMAN

VIRGILIA
Heavens bless my lord from fell Aufidius!

VOLUMNIA
He'll beat Aufidius 'head below his knee
And tread upon his neck.

Enter VALERIA, with an USHER and GENTLEWOMAN

VALERIA
My ladies both, good day to you.

VOLUMNIA
Sweet madam.

VIRGILIA
I am glad to see your ladyship.

VALERIA
How do you both? you are manifest house-keepers.
What are you sewing here? A fine spot, in good faith. How does your little son?

VIRGILIA
I thank your ladyship; well, good madam.

VOLUMNIA
He had rather see the swords, and hear a drum, than look upon his school-master.

VALERIA
O' my word, the father's son: I'll swear, 'tis a very pretty boy. O' my troth, I looked upon him o' Wednesday half an hour together: has such a confirmed countenance. I saw him run after a gilded butterfly: and when he caught it, he let it go again; and after it again; and over and over he comes, and again; catched it again; or whether his fall enraged him, or how 'twas, he did so set his teeth and tear it; O, I warrant it, how he mammocked it!

VOLUMNIA
One on 's father's moods.

VALERIA
Indeed, la, 'tis a noble child.

VIRGILIA
A crack, madam.

VALERIA
Come, lay aside your stitchery; I must have you play the idle husewife with me this afternoon.

VIRGILIA
No, good madam; I will not out of doors.

VALERIA
Not out of doors!

VOLUMNIA
She shall, she shall.

VIRGILIA
Indeed, no, by your patience; I'll not over the threshold till my lord return from the wars.

VALERIA
Fie, you confine yourself most unreasonably: come, you must go visit the good lady that lies in.

VIRGILIA
I will wish her speedy strength, and visit her with my prayers; but I cannot go thither.

VOLUMNIA
Why, I pray you?

VIRGILIA
'Tis not to save labour, nor that I want love.

VALERIA
You would be another Penelope: yet, they say, all the yarn she spun in Ulysses' absence did but fill Ithaca full of moths. Come; I would your cambric were sensible as your finger, that you might leave pricking it for pity. Come, you shall go with us.

VIRGILIA
No, good madam, pardon me; indeed, I will not forth.

VALERIA
In truth, la, go with me; and I'll tell you excellent news of your husband.

VIRGILIA
O, good madam, there can be none yet.

VALERIA
Verily, I do not jest with you; there came news from him last night.

VIRGILIA
Indeed, madam?

VALERIA
In earnest, it's true; I heard a senator speak it. Thus it is: the Volsces have an army forth; against whom Cominius the general is gone, with one part of our Roman power: your lord and Titus Lartius are set down before their city Corioli; they nothing doubt prevailing and to make it brief wars. This is true, on mine honour; and so, I pray, go with us.

VIRGILIA
Give me excuse, good madam; I will obey you in every thing hereafter.

VOLUMNIA
Let her alone, lady: as she is now, she will but disease our better mirth.

VALERIA
In troth, I think she would. Fare you well, then. Come, good sweet lady. Prithee, Virgilia, turn thy solemness out o' door. and go along with us.

VIRGILIA
No, at a word, madam; indeed, I must not. I wish you much mirth.

VALERIA
Well, then, farewell.

Exeunt

SCENE IV. Before Corioli.

Enter, with drum and colours, MARCIUS, TITUS LARTIUS, Captains and Soldiers. To them a MESSENGER

MARCIUS
Yonder comes news. A wager they have met.

LARTIUS
My horse to yours, no.

MARCIUS
'Tis done.

LARTIUS
Agreed.

MARCIUS
Say, has our general met the enemy?

MESSENGER
They lie in view; but have not spoke as yet.

LARTIUS
So, the good horse is mine.

MARCIUS
I'll buy him of you.

LARTIUS
No, I'll nor sell nor give him: lend you him I will
For half a hundred years. Summon the town.

MARCIUS
How far off lie these armies?

MESSENGER
Within this mile and half.

MARCIUS
Then shall we hear their 'larum, and they ours.
Now, Mars, I prithee, make us quick in work,
That we with smoking swords may march from hence,
To help our fielded friends! Come, blow thy blast.

They sound a parley. Enter two SENATORS with others on the walls

Tutus Aufidius, is he within your walls?

FIRST SENATOR
No, nor a man that fears you less than he,
That's lesser than a little.

Drums afar off

Hark! our drums
Are bringing forth our youth. We'll break our walls,
Rather than they shall pound us up: our gates,
Which yet seem shut, we, have but pinn'd with rushes;
They'll open of themselves.

Alarum afar off

Hark you. far off!
There is Aufidius; list, what work he makes
Amongst your cloven army.

MARCIUS
O, they are at it!

LARTIUS
Their noise be our instruction. Ladders, ho!

Enter the army of the Volsces

MARCIUS
They fear us not, but issue forth their city.
Now put your shields before your hearts, and fight
With hearts more proof than shields. Advance, brave Titus:
They do disdain us much beyond our thoughts,
Which makes me sweat with wrath. Come on, my fellows:
He that retires I'll take him for a Volsce,
And he shall feel mine edge.

Alarum.

The Romans are beat back to their trenches. Re-enter MARCIUS cursing

MARCIUS
All the contagion of the south light on you,
You shames of Rome! you herd of—Boils and plagues
Plaster you o'er, that you may be abhorr'd
Further than seen and one infect another
Against the wind a mile! You souls of geese,
That bear the shapes of men, how have you run
From slaves that apes would beat! Pluto and hell!
All hurt behind; backs red, and faces pale
With flight and agued fear! Mend and charge home,
Or, by the fires of heaven, I'll leave the foe
And make my wars on you: look to't: come on;
If you'll stand fast, we'll beat them to their wives,
As they us to our trenches followed.

Another alarum.

The Volsces fly, and MARCIUS follows them to the gates

So, now the gates are ope: now prove good seconds:
'Tis for the followers fortune widens them,
Not for the fliers: mark me, and do the like.

Enters the gates

FIRST SOLDIER
Fool-hardiness; not I.

SECOND SOLDIER
Nor I.

MARCIUS is shut in

FIRST SOLDIER
See, they have shut him in.

ALL
To the pot, I warrant him.

Alarum continues

Re-enter TITUS LARTIUS

LARTIUS
What is become of Marcius?

ALL
Slain, sir, doubtless.

FIRST SOLDIER
Following the fliers at the very heels,
With them he enters; who, upon the sudden,
Clapp'd to their gates: he is himself alone,
To answer all the city.

LARTIUS
O noble fellow!
Who sensibly outdares his senseless sword,
And, when it bows, stands up. Thou art left, Marcius:
A carbuncle entire, as big as thou art,
Were not so rich a jewel. Thou wast a soldier
Even to Cato's wish, not fierce and terrible
Only in strokes; but, with thy grim looks and
The thunder-like percussion of thy sounds,
Thou madst thine enemies shake, as if the world
Were feverous and did tremble.

Re-enter MARCIUS, bleeding, assaulted by the enemy

FIRST SOLDIER
Look, sir.

LARTIUS
O,'tis Marcius!
Let's fetch him off, or make remain alike.

They fight, and all enter the city

SCENE V. Corioli. A Street.

Enter certain ROMANS, with spoils

FIRST ROMAN

This will I carry to Rome.

SECOND ROMAN
And I this.

THIRD ROMAN
A murrain on't! I took this for silver.

Alarum continues still afar off

Enter MARCIUS and TITUS LARTIUS with a trumpet

MARCIUS
See here these movers that do prize their hours
At a crack'd drachm! Cushions, leaden spoons,
Irons of a doit, doublets that hangmen would
Bury with those that wore them, these base slaves,
Ere yet the fight be done, pack up: down with them!
And hark, what noise the general makes! To him!
There is the man of my soul's hate, Aufidius,
Piercing our Romans: then, valiant Titus, take
Convenient numbers to make good the city;
Whilst I, with those that have the spirit, will haste
To help Cominius.

LARTIUS
Worthy sir, thou bleed'st;
Thy exercise hath been too violent for
A second course of fight.

MARCIUS
Sir, praise me not;
My work hath yet not warm'd me: fare you well:
The blood I drop is rather physical
Than dangerous to me: to Aufidius thus
I will appear, and fight.

LARTIUS
Now the fair goddess, Fortune,
Fall deep in love with thee; and her great charms
Misguide thy opposers' swords! Bold gentleman,
Prosperity be thy page!

MARCIUS
Thy friend no less
Than those she placeth highest! So, farewell.

LARTIUS
Thou worthiest Marcius!

Exit MARCIUS

Go, sound thy trumpet in the market-place;
Call thither all the officers o' the town,
Where they shall know our mind: away!

Exeunt

SCENE VI. Near the Camp of Cominius.

Enter COMINIUS, as it were in retire, with SOLDIERS

COMINIUS
Breathe you, my friends: well fought; we are come off
Like Romans, neither foolish in our stands,
Nor cowardly in retire: believe me, sirs,
We shall be charged again. Whiles we have struck,
By interims and conveying gusts we have heard
The charges of our friends. Ye Roman gods!
Lead their successes as we wish our own,
That both our powers, with smiling fronts encountering,
May give you thankful sacrifice.

Enter a MESSENGER

Thy news?

MESSENGER
The citizens of Corioli have issued,
And given to Lartius and to Marcius battle:
I saw our party to their trenches driven,
And then I came away.

COMINIUS
Though thou speak'st truth,
Methinks thou speak'st not well.
How long is't since?

MESSENGER
Above an hour, my lord.

COMINIUS
'Tis not a mile; briefly we heard their drums:
How couldst thou in a mile confound an hour,
And bring thy news so late?

MESSENGER
Spies of the Volsces
Held me in chase, that I was forced to wheel

Three or four miles about, else had I, sir,
Half an hour since brought my report.

COMINIUS
Who's yonder,
That does appear as he were flay'd? O gods
He has the stamp of Marcius; and I have
Before-time seen him thus.

MARCIUS
[Within] Come I too late?

COMINIUS
The shepherd knows not thunder from a tabour
More than I know the sound of Marcius' tongue
From every meaner man.

Enter MARCIUS

MARCIUS
Come I too late?

COMINIUS
Ay, if you come not in the blood of others,
But mantled in your own.

MARCIUS
O, let me clip ye
In arms as sound as when I woo'd, in heart
As merry as when our nuptial day was done,
And tapers burn'd to bedward!

COMINIUS
Flower of warriors,
How is it with Titus Lartius?

MARCIUS
As with a man busied about decrees:
Condemning some to death, and some to exile;
Ransoming him, or pitying, threatening the other;
Holding Corioli in the name of Rome,
Even like a fawning greyhound in the leash,
To let him slip at will.

COMINIUS
Where is that slave
Which told me they had beat you to your trenches?
Where is he? call him hither.

MARCIUS

Let him alone;
He did inform the truth: but for our gentlemen,
The common file—a plague! tribunes for them!—
The mouse ne'er shunn'd the cat as they did budge
From rascals worse than they.

COMINIUS
But how prevail'd you?

MARCIUS
Will the time serve to tell? I do not think.
Where is the enemy? are you lords o' the field?
If not, why cease you till you are so?

COMINIUS
Marcius,
We have at disadvantage fought and did
Retire to win our purpose.

MARCIUS
How lies their battle? know you on which side
They have placed their men of trust?

COMINIUS
As I guess, Marcius,
Their bands i' the vaward are the Antiates,
Of their best trust; o'er them Aufidius,
Their very heart of hope.

MARCIUS
I do beseech you,
By all the battles wherein we have fought,
By the blood we have shed together, by the vows
We have made to endure friends, that you directly
Set me against Aufidius and his Antiates;
And that you not delay the present, but,
Filling the air with swords advanced and darts,
We prove this very hour.

COMINIUS
Though I could wish
You were conducted to a gentle bath
And balms applied to, you, yet dare I never
Deny your asking: take your choice of those
That best can aid your action.

MARCIUS
Those are they
That most are willing. If any such be here—
As it were sin to doubt—that love this painting
Wherein you see me smear'd; if any fear

Lesser his person than an ill report;
If any think brave death outweighs bad life
And that his country's dearer than himself;
Let him alone, or so many so minded,
Wave thus, to express his disposition,
And follow Marcius.

They all shout and wave their swords, take him up in their arms, and cast up their caps

O, me alone! make you a sword of me?
If these shows be not outward, which of you
But is four Volsces? none of you but is
Able to bear against the great Aufidius
A shield as hard as his. A certain number,
Though thanks to all, must I select from all: the rest
Shall bear the business in some other fight,
As cause will be obey'd. Please you to march;
And four shall quickly draw out my command,
Which men are best inclined.

COMINIUS
March on, my fellows:
Make good this ostentation, and you shall
Divide in all with us.

Exeunt

SCENE VII. The Gates of Corioli.

TITUS LARTIUS, having set a guard upon Corioli, going with drum and trumpet toward COMINIUS and CAIUS MARCIUS, enters with Lieutenant, other Soldiers, and a Scout

LARTIUS
So, let the ports be guarded: keep your duties,
As I have set them down. If I do send, dispatch
Those centuries to our aid: the rest will serve
For a short holding: if we lose the field,
We cannot keep the town.

LIEUTENANT
Fear not our care, sir.

LARTIUS
Hence, and shut your gates upon's.
Our guider, come; to the Roman camp conduct us.

Exeunt

SCENE VIII. A Field of Battle.

Alarum as in battle. Enter, from opposite sides, MARCIUS and AUFIDIUS

MARCIUS
I'll fight with none but thee; for I do hate thee
Worse than a promise-breaker.

AUFIDIUS
We hate alike:
Not Afric owns a serpent I abhor
More than thy fame and envy. Fix thy foot.

MARCIUS
Let the first budger die the other's slave,
And the gods doom him after!

AUFIDIUS
If I fly, Marcius,
Holloa me like a hare.

MARCIUS
Within these three hours, Tullus,
Alone I fought in your Corioli walls,
And made what work I pleased: 'tis not my blood
Wherein thou seest me mask'd; for thy revenge
Wrench up thy power to the highest.

AUFIDIUS
Wert thou the Hector
That was the whip of your bragg'd progeny,
Thou shouldst not scape me here.

They fight, and certain Volsces come to the aid of AUFIDIUS. MARCIUS fights till they be driven in breathless

Officious, and not valiant, you have shamed me
In your condemned seconds.

Exeunt

SCENE IX. The Roman Camp.

Flourish. Alarum.

A retreat is sounded. Flourish. Enter, from one side, COMINIUS with the Romans; from the other side, MARCIUS, with his arm in a scarf

COMINIUS

If I should tell thee o'er this thy day's work,
Thou'ldst not believe thy deeds: but I'll report it
Where senators shall mingle tears with smiles,
Where great patricians shall attend and shrug,
I' the end admire, where ladies shall be frighted,
And, gladly quaked, hear more; where the dull tribunes,
That, with the fusty plebeians, hate thine honours,
Shall say against their hearts 'We thank the gods
Our Rome hath such a soldier.'
Yet camest thou to a morsel of this feast,
Having fully dined before.

Enter TITUS LARTIUS, with his power, from the pursuit

LARTIUS
O general,
Here is the steed, we the caparison:
Hadst thou beheld

MARCIUS
Pray now, no more: my mother,
Who has a charter to extol her blood,
When she does praise me grieves me. I have done
As you have done; that's what I can; induced
As you have been; that's for my country:
He that has but effected his good will
Hath overta'en mine act.

COMINIUS
You shall not be
The grave of your deserving; Rome must know
The value of her own: 'twere a concealment
Worse than a theft, no less than a traducement,
To hide your doings; and to silence that,
Which, to the spire and top of praises vouch'd,
Would seem but modest: therefore, I beseech you
In sign of what you are, not to reward
What you have done—before our army hear me.

MARCIUS
I have some wounds upon me, and they smart
To hear themselves remember'd.

COMINIUS
Should they not,
Well might they fester 'gainst ingratitude,
And tent themselves with death. Of all the horses,
Whereof we have ta'en good and good store, of all
The treasure in this field achieved and city,
We render you the tenth, to be ta'en forth,

Before the common distribution, at
Your only choice.

MARCIUS
I thank you, general;
But cannot make my heart consent to take
A bribe to pay my sword: I do refuse it;
And stand upon my common part with those
That have beheld the doing.

A long flourish.

They all cry 'Marcius! Marcius!' cast up their caps and lances: COMINIUS and LARTIUS stand bare

MARCIUS
May these same instruments, which you profane,
Never sound more! when drums and trumpets shall
I' the field prove flatterers, let courts and cities be
Made all of false-faced soothing!
When steel grows soft as the parasite's silk,
Let him be made a coverture for the wars!
No more, I say! For that I have not wash'd
My nose that bled, or foil'd some debile wretch.—
Which, without note, here's many else have done,—
You shout me forth
In acclamations hyperbolical;
As if I loved my little should be dieted
In praises sauced with lies.

COMINIUS
Too modest are you;
More cruel to your good report than grateful
To us that give you truly: by your patience,
If 'gainst yourself you be incensed, we'll put you,
Like one that means his proper harm, in manacles,
Then reason safely with you. Therefore, be it known,
As to us, to all the world, that Caius Marcius
Wears this war's garland: in token of the which,
My noble steed, known to the camp, I give him,
With all his trim belonging; and from this time,
For what he did before Corioli, call him,
With all the applause and clamour of the host,
CAIUS MARCIUS CORIOLANUS! Bear
The addition nobly ever!

Flourish. Trumpets sound, and drums

ALL
Caius Marcius Coriolanus!

CORIOLANUS

I will go wash;
And when my face is fair, you shall perceive
Whether I blush or no: howbeit, I thank you.
I mean to stride your steed, and at all times
To undercrest your good addition
To the fairness of my power.

COMINIUS
So, to our tent;
Where, ere we do repose us, we will write
To Rome of our success. You, Titus Lartius,
Must to Corioli back: send us to Rome
The best, with whom we may articulate,
For their own good and ours.

LARTIUS
I shall, my lord.

CORIOLANUS
The gods begin to mock me. I, that now
Refused most princely gifts, am bound to beg
Of my lord general.

COMINIUS
Take't; 'tis yours. What is't?

CORIOLANUS
I sometime lay here in Corioli
At a poor man's house; he used me kindly:
He cried to me; I saw him prisoner;
But then Aufidius was with in my view,
And wrath o'erwhelm'd my pity: I request you
To give my poor host freedom.

COMINIUS
O, well begg'd!
Were he the butcher of my son, he should
Be free as is the wind. Deliver him, Titus.

LARTIUS
Marcius, his name?

CORIOLANUS
By Jupiter! forgot.
I am weary; yea, my memory is tired.
Have we no wine here?

COMINIUS
Go we to our tent:
The blood upon your visage dries; 'tis time
It should be look'd to: come.

Exeunt

SCENE X. The Camp of the Volsces.

A flourish. Cornets. Enter TULLUS AUFIDIUS, bloody, with two or three SOLDIERS

AUFIDIUS
The town is ta'en!

FIRST SOLDIER
'Twill be deliver'd back on good condition.

AUFIDIUS
Condition!
I would I were a Roman; for I cannot,
Being a Volsce, be that I am. Condition!
What good condition can a treaty find
I' the part that is at mercy? Five times, Marcius,
I have fought with thee: so often hast thou beat me,
And wouldst do so, I think, should we encounter
As often as we eat. By the elements,
If e'er again I meet him beard to beard,
He's mine, or I am his: mine emulation
Hath not that honour in't it had; for where
I thought to crush him in an equal force,
True sword to sword, I'll potch at him some way
Or wrath or craft may get him.

FIRST SOLDIER
He's the devil.

AUFIDIUS
Bolder, though not so subtle. My valour's poison'd
With only suffering stain by him; for him
Shall fly out of itself: nor sleep nor sanctuary,
Being naked, sick, nor fane nor Capitol,
The prayers of priests nor times of sacrifice,
Embarquements all of fury, shall lift up
Their rotten privilege and custom 'gainst
My hate to Marcius: where I find him, were it
At home, upon my brother's guard, even there,
Against the hospitable canon, would I
Wash my fierce hand in's heart. Go you to the city;
Learn how 'tis held; and what they are that must
Be hostages for Rome.

FIRST SOLDIER
Will not you go?

AUFIDIUS
I am attended at the cypress grove: I pray you—
'Tis south the city mills—bring me word thither
How the world goes, that to the pace of it
I may spur on my journey.

FIRST SOLDIER
I shall, sir.

Exeunt

ACT II

SCENE I. Rome. A Public Place.

Enter MENENIUS with the two Tribunes of the people, SICINIUS and BRUTUS.

MENENIUS
The augurer tells me we shall have news to-night.

BRUTUS
Good or bad?

MENENIUS
Not according to the prayer of the people, for they love not Marcius.

SICINIUS
Nature teaches beasts to know their friends.

MENENIUS
Pray you, who does the wolf love?

SICINIUS
The lamb.

MENENIUS
Ay, to devour him; as the hungry plebeians would the noble Marcius.

BRUTUS
He's a lamb indeed, that baes like a bear.

MENENIUS
He's a bear indeed, that lives like a lamb. You two are old men: tell me one thing that I shall ask you.

BOTH
Well, sir.

MENENIUS

In what enormity is Marcius poor in, that you two have not in abundance?

BRUTUS
He's poor in no one fault, but stored with all.

SICINIUS
Especially in pride.

BRUTUS
And topping all others in boasting.

MENENIUS
This is strange now: do you two know how you are censured here in the city, I mean of us o' the right-hand file? do you?

BOTH
Why, how are we censured?

MENENIUS
Because you talk of pride now,—will you not be angry?

BOTH
Well, well, sir, well.

MENENIUS
Why, 'tis no great matter; for a very little thief of occasion will rob you of a great deal of patience: give your dispositions the reins, and be angry at your pleasures; at the least if you take it as a pleasure to you in being so. You blame Marcius for being proud?

BRUTUS
We do it not alone, sir.

MENENIUS
I know you can do very little alone; for your helps are many, or else your actions would grow wondrous single: your abilities are too infant-like for doing much alone. You talk of pride: O that you could turn your eyes toward the napes of your necks, and make but an interior survey of your good selves! O that you could!

BRUTUS
What then, sir?

MENENIUS
Why, then you should discover a brace of unmeriting, proud, violent, testy magistrates, alias fools, as any in Rome.

SICINIUS
Menenius, you are known well enough too.

MENENIUS
I am known to be a humorous patrician, and one that loves a cup of hot wine with not a drop of allaying Tiber in't; said to be something imperfect in favouring the first complaint; hasty and tinder-

like upon too trivial motion; one that converses more with the buttock of the night than with the forehead of the morning: what I think I utter, and spend my malice in my breath. Meeting two such wealsmen as you are I cannot call you Lycurguses—if the drink you give me touch my palate adversely, I make a crooked face at it. I can't say your worships have delivered the matter well, when I find the ass in compound with the major part of your syllables: and though I must be content to bear with those that say you are reverend grave men, yet they lie deadly that tell you you have good faces. If you see this in the map of my microcosm, follows it that I am known well enough too? what barm can your bison conspectuities glean out of this character, if I be known well enough too?

BRUTUS
Come, sir, come, we know you well enough.

MENENIUS
You know neither me, yourselves nor any thing. You are ambitious for poor knaves' caps and legs: you wear out a good wholesome forenoon in hearing a cause between an orange wife and a fosset-seller; and then rejourn the controversy of three pence to a second day of audience. When you are hearing a matter between party and party, if you chance to be pinched with the colic, you make faces like mummers; set up the bloody flag against all patience; and, in roaring for a chamber-pot, dismiss the controversy bleeding the more entangled by your hearing: all the peace you make in their cause is, calling both the parties knaves. You are a pair of strange ones.

BRUTUS
Come, come, you are well understood to be a perfecter giber for the table than a necessary bencher in the Capitol.

MENENIUS
Our very priests must become mockers, if they shall encounter such ridiculous subjects as you are. When you speak best unto the purpose, it is not worth the wagging of your beards; and your beards deserve not so honourable a grave as to stuff a botcher's cushion, or to be entombed in an ass's pack-saddle. Yet you must be saying, Marcius is proud; who in a cheap estimation, is worth predecessors since Deucalion, though peradventure some of the best of 'em were hereditary hangmen. God-den to your worships: more of your conversation would infect my brain, being the herdsmen of the beastly plebeians: I will be bold to take my leave of you.

BRUTUS and SICINIUS go aside

Enter VOLUMNIA, VIRGILIA, and VALERIA

How now, my as fair as noble ladies,—and the moon, were she earthly, no nobler,—whither do you follow your eyes so fast?

VOLUMNIA
Honourable Menenius, my boy Marcius approaches; for the love of Juno, let's go.

MENENIUS
Ha! Marcius coming home!

VOLUMNIA
Ay, worthy Menenius; and with most prosperous approbation.

MENENIUS

Take my cap, Jupiter, and I thank thee. Hoo!
Marcius coming home!

VOLUMNIA VIRGILIA
Nay,'tis true.

VOLUMNIA
Look, here's a letter from him: the state hath another, his wife another; and, I think, there's one at home for you.

MENENIUS
I will make my very house reel tonight: a letter for me!

VIRGILIA
Yes, certain, there's a letter for you; I saw't.

MENENIUS
A letter for me! it gives me an estate of seven years' health; in which time I will make a lip at the physician: the most sovereign prescription in Galen is but empiricutic, and, to this preservative, of no better report than a horse-drench. Is he not wounded? he was wont to come home wounded.

VIRGILIA
O, no, no, no.

VOLUMNIA
O, he is wounded; I thank the gods for't.

MENENIUS
So do I too, if it be not too much: brings a' victory in his pocket? the wounds become him.

VOLUMNIA
On's brows: Menenius, he comes the third time home with the oaken garland.

MENENIUS
Has he disciplined Aufidius soundly?

VOLUMNIA
Titus Lartius writes, they fought together, but
Aufidius got off.

MENENIUS
And 'twas time for him too, I'll warrant him that: an he had stayed by him, I would not have been so fidiused for all the chests in Corioli, and the gold that's in them. Is the senate possessed of this?

VOLUMNIA
Good ladies, let's go. Yes, yes, yes; the senate has letters from the general, wherein he gives my son the whole name of the war: he hath in this action outdone his former deeds doubly

VALERIA
In troth, there's wondrous things spoke of him.

MENENIUS
Wondrous! ay, I warrant you, and not without his true purchasing.

VIRGILIA
The gods grant them true!

VOLUMNIA
True! pow, wow.

MENENIUS
True! I'll be sworn they are true.
Where is he wounded?

To the Tribunes

God save your good worships! Marcius is coming home: he has more cause to be proud. Where is he wounded?

VOLUMNIA
I' the shoulder and i' the left arm there will be large cicatrices to show the people, when he shall stand for his place. He received in the repulse of Tarquin seven hurts i' the body.

MENENIUS
One i' the neck, and two i' the thigh,—there's nine that I know.

VOLUMNIA
He had, before this last expedition, twenty-five wounds upon him.

MENENIUS
Now it's twenty-seven: every gash was an enemy's grave.

A shout and flourish

Hark! the trumpets.

VOLUMNIA
These are the ushers of Marcius: before him he carries noise, and behind him he leaves tears: Death, that dark spirit, in 's nervy arm doth lie; Which, being advanced, declines, and then men die.

A sennet. Trumpets sound.

Enter COMINIUS the general, and TITUS LARTIUS; between them, CORIOLANUS, crowned with an oaken garland; with Captains and Soldiers, and a Herald

HERALD
Know, Rome, that all alone Marcius did fight
Within Corioli gates: where he hath won,
With fame, a name to Caius Marcius; these
In honour follows Coriolanus.
Welcome to Rome, renowned Coriolanus!

Flourish

ALL
Welcome to Rome, renowned Coriolanus!

CORIOLANUS
No more of this; it does offend my heart:
Pray now, no more.

COMINIUS
Look, sir, your mother!

CORIOLANUS
O, You have, I know, petition'd all the gods
For my prosperity!

Kneels

VOLUMNIA
Nay, my good soldier, up;
My gentle Marcius, worthy Caius, and
By deed-achieving honour newly named,—
What is it?—Coriolanus must I call thee?—
But O, thy wife!

CORIOLANUS
My gracious silence, hail!
Wouldst thou have laugh'd had I come coffin'd home,
That weep'st to see me triumph? Ay, my dear,
Such eyes the widows in Corioli wear,
And mothers that lack sons.

MENENIUS
Now, the gods crown thee!

CORIOLANUS
And live you yet?

To VALERIA

O my sweet lady, pardon.

VOLUMNIA
I know not where to turn: O, welcome home:
And welcome, general: and ye're welcome all.

MENENIUS
A hundred thousand welcomes. I could weep
And I could laugh, I am light and heavy. Welcome.
A curse begin at very root on's heart,
That is not glad to see thee! You are three

That Rome should dote on: yet, by the faith of men,
We have some old crab-trees here
at home that will not
Be grafted to your relish. Yet welcome, warriors:
We call a nettle but a nettle and
The faults of fools but folly.

COMINIUS
Ever right.

CORIOLANUS
Menenius ever, ever.

Herald
Give way there, and go on!

CORIOLANUS
[To VOLUMNIA and VIRGILIA] Your hand, and yours:
Ere in our own house I do shade my head,
The good patricians must be visited;
From whom I have received not only greetings,
But with them change of honours.

VOLUMNIA
I have lived
To see inherited my very wishes
And the buildings of my fancy: only
There's one thing wanting, which I doubt not but
Our Rome will cast upon thee.

CORIOLANUS
Know, good mother,
I had rather be their servant in my way,
Than sway with them in theirs.

COMINIUS
On, to the Capitol!

Flourish. Cornets.

Exeunt in state, as before. BRUTUS and SICINIUS come forward

BRUTUS
All tongues speak of him, and the bleared sights
Are spectacled to see him: your prattling nurse
Into a rapture lets her baby cry
While she chats him: the kitchen malkin pins
Her richest lockram 'bout her reechy neck,
Clambering the walls to eye him: stalls, bulks, windows,
Are smother'd up, leads fill'd, and ridges horsed
With variable complexions, all agreeing

In earnestness to see him: seld-shown flamens
Do press among the popular throngs and puff
To win a vulgar station: or veil'd dames
Commit the war of white and damask in
Their nicely-gawded cheeks to the wanton spoil
Of Phoebus' burning kisses: such a pother
As if that whatsoever god who leads him
Were slily crept into his human powers
And gave him graceful posture.

SICINIUS
On the sudden,
I warrant him consul.

BRUTUS
Then our office may,
During his power, go sleep.

SICINIUS
He cannot temperately transport his honours
From where he should begin and end, but will
Lose those he hath won.

BRUTUS
In that there's comfort.

SICINIUS
Doubt not
The commoners, for whom we stand, but they
Upon their ancient malice will forget
With the least cause these his new honours, which
That he will give them make I as little question
As he is proud to do't.

BRUTUS
I heard him swear,
Were he to stand for consul, never would he
Appear i' the market-place nor on him put
The napless vesture of humility;
Nor showing, as the manner is, his wounds
To the people, beg their stinking breaths.

SICINIUS
'Tis right.

BRUTUS
It was his word: O, he would miss it rather
Than carry it but by the suit of the gentry to him,
And the desire of the nobles.

SICINIUS

I wish no better
Than have him hold that purpose and to put it
In execution.

BRUTUS
'Tis most like he will.

SICINIUS
It shall be to him then as our good wills,
A sure destruction.

BRUTUS
So it must fall out
To him or our authorities. For an end,
We must suggest the people in what hatred
He still hath held them; that to's power he would
Have made them mules, silenced their pleaders and
Dispropertied their freedoms, holding them,
In human action and capacity,
Of no more soul nor fitness for the world
Than camels in the war, who have their provand
Only for bearing burdens, and sore blows
For sinking under them.

SICINIUS
This, as you say, suggested
At some time when his soaring insolence
Shall touch the people—which time shall not want,
If he be put upon 't; and that's as easy
As to set dogs on sheep—will be his fire
To kindle their dry stubble; and their blaze
Shall darken him for ever.

Enter a MESSENGER

BRUTUS
What's the matter?

MESSENGER
You are sent for to the Capitol. 'Tis thought
That Marcius shall be consul:
I have seen the dumb men throng to see him and
The blind to bear him speak: matrons flung gloves,
Ladies and maids their scarfs and handkerchers,
Upon him as he pass'd: the nobles bended,
As to Jove's statue, and the commons made
A shower and thunder with their caps and shouts:
I never saw the like.

BRUTUS

Let's to the Capitol;
And carry with us ears and eyes for the time,
But hearts for the event.

SICINIUS
Have with you.

Exeunt

SCENE II. The Same. The Capitol.

Enter two OFFICERS, to lay cushions

FIRST OFFICER
Come, come, they are almost here. How many stand for consulships?

SECOND OFFICER
Three, they say: but 'tis thought of every one Coriolanus will carry it.

FIRST OFFICER
That's a brave fellow; but he's vengeance proud, and loves not the common people.

SECOND OFFICER
Faith, there had been many great men that have flattered the people, who ne'er loved them; and there be many that they have loved, they know not wherefore: so that, if they love they know not why, they hate upon no better a ground: therefore, for Coriolanus neither to care whether they love or hate him manifests the true knowledge he has in their disposition; and out of his noble carelessness lets them plainly see't.

FIRST OFFICER
If he did not care whether he had their love or no, he waved indifferently 'twixt doing them neither good nor harm: but he seeks their hate with greater devotion than can render it him; and leaves nothing undone that may fully discover him their opposite. Now, to seem to affect the malice and displeasure of the people is as bad as that which he dislikes, to flatter them for their love.

SECOND OFFICER
He hath deserved worthily of his country: and his ascent is not by such easy degrees as those who, having been supple and courteous to the people, bonneted, without any further deed to have them at an into their estimation and report: but he hath so planted his honours in their eyes, and his actions in their hearts, that for their tongues to be silent, and not confess so much, were a kind of ingrateful injury; to report otherwise, were a malice, that, giving itself the lie, would pluck reproof and rebuke from every ear that heard it.

FIRST OFFICER
No more of him; he is a worthy man: make way, they are coming.

A sennet.

Enter, with actors before them, COMINIUS the consul, MENENIUS, CORIOLANUS, Senators, SICINIUS and BRUTUS. The Senators take their places; the Tribunes take their Places by themselves. CORIOLANUS stands

MENENIUS
Having determined of the Volsces and
To send for Titus Lartius, it remains,
As the main point of this our after-meeting,
To gratify his noble service that
Hath thus stood for his country: therefore, please you,
Most reverend and grave elders, to desire
The present consul, and last general
In our well-found successes, to report
A little of that worthy work perform'd
By Caius Marcius Coriolanus, whom
We met here both to thank and to remember
With honours like himself.

FIRST SENATOR
Speak, good Cominius:
Leave nothing out for length, and make us think
Rather our state's defective for requital
Than we to stretch it out.

To the Tribunes

Masters o' the people,
We do request your kindest ears, and after,
Your loving motion toward the common body,
To yield what passes here.

SICINIUS
We are convented
Upon a pleasing treaty, and have hearts
Inclinable to honour and advance
The theme of our assembly.

BRUTUS
Which the rather
We shall be blest to do, if he remember
A kinder value of the people than
He hath hereto prized them at.

MENENIUS
That's off, that's off;
I would you rather had been silent. Please you
To hear Cominius speak?

BRUTUS

Most willingly;
But yet my caution was more pertinent
Than the rebuke you give it.

MENENIUS
He loves your people
But tie him not to be their bedfellow.
Worthy Cominius, speak.

CORIOLANUS offers to go away

Nay, keep your place.

FIRST SENATOR
Sit, Coriolanus; never shame to hear
What you have nobly done.

CORIOLANUS
Your horror's pardon:
I had rather have my wounds to heal again
Than hear say how I got them.

BRUTUS
Sir, I hope
My words disbench'd you not.

CORIOLANUS
No, sir: yet oft,
When blows have made me stay, I fled from words.
You soothed not, therefore hurt not: but your people,
I love them as they weigh.

MENENIUS
Pray now, sit down.

CORIOLANUS
I had rather have one scratch my head i' the sun
When the alarum were struck than idly sit
To hear my nothings monster'd.

Exit

MENENIUS
Masters of the people,
Your multiplying spawn how can he flatter—
That's thousand to one good one—when you now see
He had rather venture all his limbs for honour
Than one on's ears to hear it? Proceed, Cominius.

COMINIUS

I shall lack voice: the deeds of Coriolanus
Should not be utter'd feebly. It is held
That valour is the chiefest virtue, and
Most dignifies the haver: if it be,
The man I speak of cannot in the world
Be singly counterpoised. At sixteen years,
When Tarquin made a head for Rome, he fought
Beyond the mark of others: our then dictator,
Whom with all praise I point at, saw him fight,
When with his Amazonian chin he drove
The bristled lips before him: be bestrid
An o'er-press'd Roman and i' the consul's view
Slew three opposers: Tarquin's self he met,
And struck him on his knee: in that day's feats,
When he might act the woman in the scene,
He proved best man i' the field, and for his meed
Was brow-bound with the oak. His pupil age
Man-enter'd thus, he waxed like a sea,
And in the brunt of seventeen battles since
He lurch'd all swords of the garland. For this last,
Before and in Corioli, let me say,
I cannot speak him home: he stopp'd the fliers;
And by his rare example made the coward
Turn terror into sport: as weeds before
A vessel under sail, so men obey'd
And fell below his stem: his sword, death's stamp,
Where it did mark, it took; from face to foot
He was a thing of blood, whose every motion
Was timed with dying cries: alone he enter'd
The mortal gate of the city, which he painted
With shunless destiny; aidless came off,
And with a sudden reinforcement struck
Corioli like a planet: now all's his:
When, by and by, the din of war gan pierce
His ready sense; then straight his doubled spirit
Re-quicken'd what in flesh was fatigate,
And to the battle came he; where he did
Run reeking o'er the lives of men, as if
'Twere a perpetual spoil: and till we call'd
Both field and city ours, he never stood
To ease his breast with panting.

MENENIUS
Worthy man!

First Senator
He cannot but with measure fit the honours
Which we devise him.

COMINIUS

Our spoils he kick'd at,
And look'd upon things precious as they were
The common muck of the world: he covets less
Than misery itself would give; rewards
His deeds with doing them, and is content
To spend the time to end it.

MENENIUS
He's right noble:
Let him be call'd for.

First Senator
Call Coriolanus.

Officer
He doth appear.

Re-enter CORIOLANUS

MENENIUS
The senate, Coriolanus, are well pleased
To make thee consul.

CORIOLANUS
I do owe them still
My life and services.

MENENIUS
It then remains
That you do speak to the people.

CORIOLANUS
I do beseech you,
Let me o'erleap that custom, for I cannot
Put on the gown, stand naked and entreat them,
For my wounds' sake, to give their suffrage: please you
That I may pass this doing.

SICINIUS
Sir, the people
Must have their voices; neither will they bate
One jot of ceremony.

MENENIUS
Put them not to't:
Pray you, go fit you to the custom and
Take to you, as your predecessors have,
Your honour with your form.

CORIOLANUS

It is apart
That I shall blush in acting, and might well
Be taken from the people.

BRUTUS
Mark you that?

CORIOLANUS
To brag unto them, thus I did, and thus;
Show them the unaching scars which I should hide,
As if I had received them for the hire
Of their breath only!

MENENIUS
Do not stand upon't.
We recommend to you, tribunes of the people,
Our purpose to them: and to our noble consul
Wish we all joy and honour.

SENATORS
To Coriolanus come all joy and honour!

Flourish of cornets.

Exeunt all but SICINIUS and BRUTUS

BRUTUS
You see how he intends to use the people.

SICINIUS
May they perceive's intent! He will require them,
As if he did contemn what he requested
Should be in them to give.

BRUTUS
Come, we'll inform them
Of our proceedings here: on the marketplace,
I know, they do attend us.

Exeunt

SCENE III. The Same. The Forum.

Enter seven or eight CITIZENS

FIRST CITIZEN
Once, if he do require our voices, we ought not to deny him.

SECOND CITIZEN

We may, sir, if we will.

THIRD CITIZEN
We have power in ourselves to do it, but it is a power that we have no power to do; for if he show us his wounds and tell us his deeds, we are to put our tongues into those wounds and speak for them; so, if he tell us his noble deeds, we must also tell him our noble acceptance of them. Ingratitude is monstrous, and for the multitude to be ingrateful, were to make a monster of the multitude: of the which we being members, should bring ourselves to be monstrous members.

FIRST CITIZEN
And to make us no better thought of, a little help will serve; for once we stood up about the corn, he himself stuck not to call us the many-headed multitude.

THIRD CITIZEN
We have been called so of many; not that our heads are some brown, some black, some auburn, some bald, but that our wits are so diversely coloured: and truly I think if all our wits were to issue out of one skull, they would fly east, west, north, south, and their consent of one direct way should be at once to all the points o' the compass.

SECOND CITIZEN
Think you so? Which way do you judge my wit would fly?

THIRD CITIZEN
Nay, your wit will not so soon out as another man's will; 'tis strongly wedged up in a block-head, but if it were at liberty, 'twould, sure, southward.

SECOND CITIZEN
Why that way?

THIRD CITIZEN
To lose itself in a fog, where being three parts melted away with rotten dews, the fourth would return for conscience sake, to help to get thee a wife.

Second Citizen
You are never without your tricks: you may, you may.

THIRD CITIZEN
Are you all resolved to give your voices? But that's no matter, the greater part carries it. I say, if he would incline to the people, there was never a worthier man.

Enter CORIOLANUS in a gown of humility, with MENENIUS

Here he comes, and in the gown of humility: mark his behavior. We are not to stay all together, but to come by him where he stands, by ones, by twos, and by threes. He's to make his requests by particulars; wherein every one of us has a single honour, in giving him our own voices with our own tongues: therefore follow me, and I direct you how you shall go by him.

ALL
Content, content.

Exeunt CITIZENS

MENENIUS
O sir, you are not right: have you not known
The worthiest men have done't?

CORIOLANUS
What must I say?
'I Pray, sir'—Plague upon't! I cannot bring
My tongue to such a pace:—'Look, sir, my wounds!
I got them in my country's service, when
Some certain of your brethren roar'd and ran
From the noise of our own drums.'

MENENIUS
O me, the gods!
You must not speak of that: you must desire them
To think upon you.

CORIOLANUS
Think upon me! hang 'em!
I would they would forget me, like the virtues
Which our divines lose by 'em.

MENENIUS
You'll mar all:
I'll leave you: pray you, speak to 'em, I pray you,
In wholesome manner.

Exit

CORIOLANUS
Bid them wash their faces
And keep their teeth clean.

Re-enter two of the CITIZENS

So, here comes a brace.

Re-enter a THIRD CITIZEN

You know the cause, air, of my standing here.

THIRD CITIZEN
We do, sir; tell us what hath brought you to't.

CORIOLANUS
Mine own desert.

SECOND CITIZEN
Your own desert!

CORIOLANUS
Ay, but not mine own desire.

THIRD CITIZEN
How not your own desire?

CORIOLANUS
No, sir,'twas never my desire yet to trouble the poor with begging.

THIRD CITIZEN
You must think, if we give you any thing, we hope to gain by you.

CORIOLANUS
Well then, I pray, your price o' the consulship?

FIRST CITIZEN
The price is to ask it kindly.

CORIOLANUS
Kindly! Sir, I pray, let me ha't: I have wounds to show you, which shall be yours in private. Your good voice, sir; what say you?

SECOND CITIZEN
You shall ha' it, worthy sir.

CORIOLANUS
A match, sir. There's in all two worthy voices begged. I have your alms: adieu.

THIRD CITIZEN
But this is something odd.

SECOND CITIZEN
An 'twere to give again,—but 'tis no matter.

Exeunt the three Citizens
Re-enter two other CITIZENS

CORIOLANUS
Pray you now, if it may stand with the tune of your voices that I may be consul, I have here the customary gown.

FOURTH CITIZEN
You have deserved nobly of your country, and you have not deserved nobly.

CORIOLANUS
Your enigma?

FOURTH CITIZEN
You have been a scourge to her enemies, you have been a rod to her friends; you have not indeed loved the common people.

CORIOLANUS
You should account me the more virtuous that I have not been common in my love. I will, sir, flatter my sworn brother, the people, to earn a dearer estimation of them; 'tis a condition they account gentle: and since the wisdom of their choice is rather to have my hat than my heart, I will practise the insinuating nod and be off to them most counterfeitly; that is, sir, I will counterfeit the bewitchment of some popular man and give it bountiful to the desirers. Therefore, beseech you, I may be consul.

FIFTH CITIZEN
We hope to find you our friend; and therefore give you our voices heartily.

FOURTH CITIZEN
You have received many wounds for your country.

CORIOLANUS
I will not seal your knowledge with showing them. I will make much of your voices, and so trouble you no further.

BOTH CITIZENS
The gods give you joy, sir, heartily!

Exeunt

CORIOLANUS
Most sweet voices!
Better it is to die, better to starve,
Than crave the hire which first we do deserve.
Why in this woolvish toge should I stand here,
To beg of Hob and Dick, that do appear,
Their needless vouches? Custom calls me to't:
What custom wills, in all things should we do't,
The dust on antique time would lie unswept,
And mountainous error be too highly heapt
For truth to o'er-peer. Rather than fool it so,
Let the high office and the honour go
To one that would do thus. I am half through;
The one part suffer'd, the other will I do.

Re-enter three CITIZENS more

Here come more voices.
Your voices: for your voices I have fought;
Watch'd for your voices; for Your voices bear
Of wounds two dozen odd; battles thrice six
I have seen and heard of; for your voices have
Done many things, some less, some more your voices:
Indeed I would be consul.

SIXTH CITIZEN
He has done nobly, and cannot go without any honest man's voice.

SEVENTH CITIZEN
Therefore let him be consul: the gods give him joy,
and make him good friend to the people!

ALL CITIZENS
Amen, amen. God save thee, noble consul!

Exeunt

CORIOLANUS
Worthy voices!

Re-enter MENENIUS, with BRUTUS and SICINIUS

MENENIUS
You have stood your limitation; and the tribunes
Endue you with the people's voice: remains
That, in the official marks invested, you
Anon do meet the senate.

CORIOLANUS
Is this done?

SICINIUS
The custom of request you have discharged:
The people do admit you, and are summon'd
To meet anon, upon your approbation.

CORIOLANUS
Where? at the senate-house?

SICINIUS
There, Coriolanus.

CORIOLANUS
May I change these garments?

SICINIUS
You may, sir.

CORIOLANUS
That I'll straight do; and, knowing myself again,
Repair to the senate-house.

MENENIUS
I'll keep you company. Will you along?

BRUTUS
We stay here for the people.

SICINIUS

Fare you well.

Exeunt CORIOLANUS and MENENIUS

He has it now, and by his looks methink
'Tis warm at 's heart.

BRUTUS
With a proud heart he wore his humble weeds.
will you dismiss the people?

Re-enter CITIZENS

SICINIUS
How now, my masters! have you chosen this man?

FIRST CITIZEN
He has our voices, sir.

BRUTUS
We pray the gods he may deserve your loves.

SECOND CITIZEN
Amen, sir: to my poor unworthy notice,
He mock'd us when he begg'd our voices.

THIRD CITIZEN
Certainly
He flouted us downright.

FIRST CITIZEN
No,'tis his kind of speech: he did not mock us.

SECOND CITIZEN
Not one amongst us, save yourself, but says
He used us scornfully: he should have show'd us
His marks of merit, wounds received for's country.

SICINIUS
Why, so he did, I am sure.

CITIZENS
No, no; no man saw 'em.

THIRD CITIZEN
He said he had wounds, which he could show in private;
And with his hat, thus waving it in scorn,
'I would be consul,' says he: 'aged custom,
But by your voices, will not so permit me;
Your voices therefore.' When we granted that,
Here was 'I thank you for your voices: thank you:

Your most sweet voices: now you have left your voices,
I have no further with you.' Was not this mockery?

SICINIUS
Why either were you ignorant to see't,
Or, seeing it, of such childish friendliness
To yield your voices?

BRUTUS
Could you not have told him
As you were lesson'd, when he had no power,
But was a petty servant to the state,
He was your enemy, ever spake against
Your liberties and the charters that you bear
I' the body of the weal; and now, arriving
A place of potency and sway o' the state,
If he should still malignantly remain
Fast foe to the plebeii, your voices might
Be curses to yourselves? You should have said
That as his worthy deeds did claim no less
Than what he stood for, so his gracious nature
Would think upon you for your voices and
Translate his malice towards you into love,
Standing your friendly lord.

SICINIUS
Thus to have said,
As you were fore-advised, had touch'd his spirit
And tried his inclination; from him pluck'd
Either his gracious promise, which you might,
As cause had call'd you up, have held him to
Or else it would have gall'd his surly nature,
Which easily endures not article
Tying him to aught; so putting him to rage,
You should have ta'en the advantage of his choler
And pass'd him unelected.

BRUTUS
Did you perceive
He did solicit you in free contempt
When he did need your loves, and do you think
That his contempt shall not be bruising to you,
When he hath power to crush? Why, had your bodies
No heart among you? or had you tongues to cry
Against the rectorship of judgment?

SICINIUS
Have you
Ere now denied the asker? and now again
Of him that did not ask, but mock, bestow
Your sued-for tongues?

THIRD CITIZEN
He's not confirm'd; we may deny him yet.

SECOND CITIZEN
And will deny him:
I'll have five hundred voices of that sound.

FIRST CITIZEN
I twice five hundred and their friends to piece 'em.

BRUTUS
Get you hence instantly, and tell those friends,
They have chose a consul that will from them take
Their liberties; make them of no more voice
Than dogs that are as often beat for barking
As therefore kept to do so.

SICINIUS
Let them assemble,
And on a safer judgment all revoke
Your ignorant election; enforce his pride,
And his old hate unto you; besides, forget not
With what contempt he wore the humble weed,
How in his suit he scorn'd you; but your loves,
Thinking upon his services, took from you
The apprehension of his present portance,
Which most gibingly, ungravely, he did fashion
After the inveterate hate he bears you.

BRUTUS
Lay
A fault on us, your tribunes; that we laboured,
No impediment between, but that you must
Cast your election on him.

SICINIUS
Say, you chose him
More after our commandment than as guided
By your own true affections, and that your minds,
Preoccupied with what you rather must do
Than what you should, made you against the grain
To voice him consul: lay the fault on us.

BRUTUS
Ay, spare us not. Say we read lectures to you.
How youngly he began to serve his country,
How long continued, and what stock he springs of,
The noble house o' the Marcians, from whence came
That Ancus Marcius, Numa's daughter's son,
Who, after great Hostilius, here was king;

Of the same house Publius and Quintus were,
That our beat water brought by conduits hither;
And [Censorinus,] nobly named so,
Twice being [by the people chosen] censor,
Was his great ancestor.

SICINIUS
One thus descended,
That hath beside well in his person wrought
To be set high in place, we did commend
To your remembrances: but you have found,
Scaling his present bearing with his past,
That he's your fixed enemy, and revoke
Your sudden approbation.

BRUTUS
Say, you ne'er had done't—
Harp on that still—but by our putting on;
And presently, when you have drawn your number,
Repair to the Capitol.

ALL
We will so: almost all
Repent in their election.

Exeunt CITIZENS

BRUTUS
Let them go on;
This mutiny were better put in hazard,
Than stay, past doubt, for greater:
If, as his nature is, he fall in rage
With their refusal, both observe and answer
The vantage of his anger.

SICINIUS
To the Capitol, come:
We will be there before the stream o' the people;
And this shall seem, as partly 'tis, their own,
Which we have goaded onward.

Exeunt

ACT III

SCENE I. Rome. A Street.

Cornets.

Enter CORIOLANUS, MENENIUS, all the Gentry, COMINIUS, TITUS LARTIUS, and other Senators

CORIOLANUS
Tullus Aufidius then had made new head?

LARTIUS
He had, my lord; and that it was which caused
Our swifter composition.

CORIOLANUS
So then the Volsces stand but as at first,
Ready, when time shall prompt them, to make road
Upon's again.

COMINIUS
They are worn, lord consul, so,
That we shall hardly in our ages see
Their banners wave again.

CORIOLANUS
Saw you Aufidius?

LARTIUS
On safe-guard he came to me; and did curse
Against the Volsces, for they had so vilely
Yielded the town: he is retired to Antium.

CORIOLANUS
Spoke he of me?

LARTIUS
He did, my lord.

CORIOLANUS
How? what?

LARTIUS
How often he had met you, sword to sword;
That of all things upon the earth he hated
Your person most, that he would pawn his fortunes
To hopeless restitution, so he might
Be call'd your vanquisher.

CORIOLANUS
At Antium lives he?

LARTIUS
At Antium.

CORIOLANUS

I wish I had a cause to seek him there,
To oppose his hatred fully. Welcome home.

Enter SICINIUS and BRUTUS

Behold, these are the tribunes of the people,
The tongues o' the common mouth: I do despise them;
For they do prank them in authority,
Against all noble sufferance.

SICINIUS
Pass no further.

CORIOLANUS
Ha! what is that?

BRUTUS
It will be dangerous to go on: no further.

CORIOLANUS
What makes this change?

MENENIUS
The matter?

COMINIUS
Hath he not pass'd the noble and the common?

BRUTUS
Cominius, no.

CORIOLANUS
Have I had children's voices?

First Senator
Tribunes, give way; he shall to the market-place.

BRUTUS
The people are incensed against him.

SICINIUS
Stop,
Or all will fall in broil.

CORIOLANUS
Are these your herd?
Must these have voices, that can yield them now
And straight disclaim their tongues? What are your offices?
You being their mouths, why rule you not their teeth?
Have you not set them on?

MENENIUS
Be calm, be calm.

CORIOLANUS
It is a purposed thing, and grows by plot,
To curb the will of the nobility:
Suffer't, and live with such as cannot rule
Nor ever will be ruled.

BRUTUS
Call't not a plot:
The people cry you mock'd them, and of late,
When corn was given them gratis, you repined;
Scandal'd the suppliants for the people, call'd them
Time-pleasers, flatterers, foes to nobleness.

CORIOLANUS
Why, this was known before.

BRUTUS
Not to them all.

CORIOLANUS
Have you inform'd them sithence?

BRUTUS
How! I inform them!

CORIOLANUS
You are like to do such business.

BRUTUS
Not unlike,
Each way, to better yours.

CORIOLANUS
Why then should I be consul? By yond clouds,
Let me deserve so ill as you, and make me
Your fellow tribune.

SICINIUS
You show too much of that
For which the people stir: if you will pass
To where you are bound, you must inquire your way,
Which you are out of, with a gentler spirit,
Or never be so noble as a consul,
Nor yoke with him for tribune.

MENENIUS
Let's be calm.

COMINIUS
The people are abused; set on. This paltering
Becomes not Rome, nor has Coriolanus
Deserved this so dishonour'd rub, laid falsely
I' the plain way of his merit.

CORIOLANUS
Tell me of corn!
This was my speech, and I will speak't again—

MENENIUS
Not now, not now.

FIRST SENATOR
Not in this heat, sir, now.

CORIOLANUS
Now, as I live, I will. My nobler friends,
I crave their pardons:
For the mutable, rank-scented many, let them
Regard me as I do not flatter, and
Therein behold themselves: I say again,
In soothing them, we nourish 'gainst our senate
The cockle of rebellion, insolence, sedition,
Which we ourselves have plough'd for, sow'd, and scatter'd,
By mingling them with us, the honour'd number,
Who lack not virtue, no, nor power, but that
Which they have given to beggars.

MENENIUS
Well, no more.

FIRST SENATOR
No more words, we beseech you.

CORIOLANUS
How! no more!
As for my country I have shed my blood,
Not fearing outward force, so shall my lungs
Coin words till their decay against those measles,
Which we disdain should tatter us, yet sought
The very way to catch them.

BRUTUS
You speak o' the people,
As if you were a god to punish, not
A man of their infirmity.

SICINIUS
'Twere well
We let the people know't.

MENENIUS
What, what? his choler?

CORIOLANUS
Choler!
Were I as patient as the midnight sleep,
By Jove, 'twould be my mind!

SICINIUS
It is a mind
That shall remain a poison where it is,
Not poison any further.

CORIOLANUS
Shall remain!
Hear you this Triton of the minnows? mark you
His absolute 'shall'?

COMINIUS
'Twas from the canon.

CORIOLANUS
'Shall'!
O good but most unwise patricians! why,
You grave but reckless senators, have you thus
Given Hydra here to choose an officer,
That with his peremptory 'shall,' being but
The horn and noise o' the monster's, wants not spirit
To say he'll turn your current in a ditch,
And make your channel his? If he have power
Then vail your ignorance; if none, awake
Your dangerous lenity. If you are learn'd,
Be not as common fools; if you are not,
Let them have cushions by you. You are plebeians,
If they be senators: and they are no less,
When, both your voices blended, the great'st taste
Most palates theirs. They choose their magistrate,
And such a one as he, who puts his 'shall,'
His popular 'shall' against a graver bench
Than ever frown in Greece. By Jove himself!
It makes the consuls base: and my soul aches
To know, when two authorities are up,
Neither supreme, how soon confusion
May enter 'twixt the gap of both and take
The one by the other.

COMINIUS
Well, on to the market-place.

CORIOLANUS

Whoever gave that counsel, to give forth
The corn o' the storehouse gratis, as 'twas used
Sometime in Greece,—

MENENIUS
Well, well, no more of that.

CORIOLANUS
Though there the people had more absolute power,
I say, they nourish'd disobedience, fed
The ruin of the state.

BRUTUS
Why, shall the people give
One that speaks thus their voice?

CORIOLANUS
I'll give my reasons,
More worthier than their voices. They know the corn
Was not our recompense, resting well assured
That ne'er did service for't: being press'd to the war,
Even when the navel of the state was touch'd,
They would not thread the gates. This kind of service
Did not deserve corn gratis. Being i' the war
Their mutinies and revolts, wherein they show'd
Most valour, spoke not for them: the accusation
Which they have often made against the senate,
All cause unborn, could never be the motive
Of our so frank donation. Well, what then?
How shall this bisson multitude digest
The senate's courtesy? Let deeds express
What's like to be their words: 'we did request it;
We are the greater poll, and in true fear
They gave us our demands.' Thus we debase
The nature of our seats and make the rabble
Call our cares fears; which will in time
Break ope the locks o' the senate and bring in
The crows to peck the eagles.

MENENIUS
Come, enough.

BRUTUS
Enough, with over-measure.

CORIOLANUS
No, take more:
What may be sworn by, both divine and human,
Seal what I end withal! This double worship,
Where one part does disdain with cause, the other
Insult without all reason, where gentry, title, wisdom,

Cannot conclude but by the yea and no
Of general ignorance,—it must omit
Real necessities, and give way the while
To unstable slightness: purpose so barr'd, it follows,
Nothing is done to purpose. Therefore, beseech you,—
You that will be less fearful than discreet,
That love the fundamental part of state
More than you doubt the change on't, that prefer
A noble life before a long, and wish
To jump a body with a dangerous physic
That's sure of death without it, at once pluck out
The multitudinous tongue; let them not lick
The sweet which is their poison: your dishonour
Mangles true judgment and bereaves the state
Of that integrity which should become't,
Not having the power to do the good it would,
For the in which doth control't.

BRUTUS
Has said enough.

SICINIUS
Has spoken like a traitor, and shall answer
As traitors do.

CORIOLANUS
Thou wretch, despite o'erwhelm thee!
What should the people do with these bald tribunes?
On whom depending, their obedience fails
To the greater bench: in a rebellion,
When what's not meet, but what must be, was law,
Then were they chosen: in a better hour,
Let what is meet be said it must be meet,
And throw their power i' the dust.

BRUTUS
Manifest treason!

SICINIUS
This a consul? no.

BRUTUS
The aediles, ho!

Enter an AEDILE

Let him be apprehended.

SICINIUS
Go, call the people:

Exit AEDILE

In whose name myself
Attach thee as a traitorous innovator,
A foe to the public weal: obey, I charge thee,
And follow to thine answer.

CORIOLANUS
Hence, old goat!
Senators, & C We'll surety him.

COMINIUS
Aged sir, hands off.

CORIOLANUS
Hence, rotten thing! or I shall shake thy bones
Out of thy garments.

SICINIUS
Help, ye citizens!

Enter a rabble of CITIZENS (Plebeians), with the AEDILES

MENENIUS
On both sides more respect.

SICINIUS
Here's he that would take from you all your power.

BRUTUS
Seize him, AEdiles!

CITIZENS
Down with him! down with him!
Senators, & C Weapons, weapons, weapons!

They all bustle about CORIOLANUS, crying

'Tribunes!' 'Patricians!' 'Citizens!' 'What, ho!'
'Sicinius!' 'Brutus!' 'Coriolanus!' 'Citizens!'
'Peace, peace, peace!' 'Stay, hold, peace!'

MENENIUS
What is about to be? I am out of breath;
Confusion's near; I cannot speak. You, tribunes
To the people! Coriolanus, patience!
Speak, good Sicinius.

SICINIUS
Hear me, people; peace!

CITIZENS
Let's hear our tribune: peace Speak, speak, speak.

SICINIUS
You are at point to lose your liberties:
Marcius would have all from you; Marcius,
Whom late you have named for consul.

MENENIUS
Fie, fie, fie!
This is the way to kindle, not to quench.

FIRST SENATOR
To unbuild the city and to lay all flat.

SICINIUS
What is the city but the people?

CITIZENS
True,
The people are the city.

BRUTUS
By the consent of all, we were establish'd
The people's magistrates.

CITIZENS
You so remain.

MENENIUS
And so are like to do.

COMINIUS
That is the way to lay the city flat;
To bring the roof to the foundation,
And bury all, which yet distinctly ranges,
In heaps and piles of ruin.

SICINIUS
This deserves death.

BRUTUS
Or let us stand to our authority,
Or let us lose it. We do here pronounce,
Upon the part o' the people, in whose power
We were elected theirs, Marcius is worthy
Of present death.

SICINIUS

Therefore lay hold of him;
Bear him to the rock Tarpeian, and from thence
Into destruction cast him.

BRUTUS
AEdiles, seize him!

CITIZENS
Yield, Marcius, yield!

MENENIUS
Hear me one word;
Beseech you, tribunes, hear me but a word.

AEDILE
Peace, peace!

MENENIUS
[To BRUTUS] Be that you seem, truly your
country's friend,
And temperately proceed to what you would
Thus violently redress.

BRUTUS
Sir, those cold ways,
That seem like prudent helps, are very poisonous
Where the disease is violent. Lay hands upon him,
And bear him to the rock.

CORIOLANUS
No, I'll die here.

Drawing his sword

There's some among you have beheld me fighting:
Come, try upon yourselves what you have seen me.

MENENIUS
Down with that sword! Tribunes, withdraw awhile.

BRUTUS
Lay hands upon him.

COMINIUS
Help Marcius, help,
You that be noble; help him, young and old!

CITIZENS
Down with him, down with him!

In this mutiny, the Tribunes, the AEdiles, and the People, are beat in

MENENIUS
Go, get you to your house; be gone, away!
All will be naught else.

SECOND SENATOR
Get you gone.

COMINIUS
Stand fast;
We have as many friends as enemies.

MENENIUS
Sham it be put to that?

FIRST SENATOR
The gods forbid!
I prithee, noble friend, home to thy house;
Leave us to cure this cause.

MENENIUS
For 'tis a sore upon us,
You cannot tent yourself: be gone, beseech you.

COMINIUS
Come, sir, along with us.

CORIOLANUS
I would they were barbarians—as they are,
Though in Rome litter'd—not Romans—as they are not,
Though calved i' the porch o' the Capitol—

MENENIUS
Be gone;
Put not your worthy rage into your tongue;
One time will owe another.

CORIOLANUS
On fair ground
I could beat forty of them.

COMINIUS
I could myself
Take up a brace o' the best of them; yea, the two tribunes:
But now 'tis odds beyond arithmetic;
And manhood is call'd foolery, when it stands
Against a falling fabric. Will you hence,
Before the tag return? whose rage doth rend
Like interrupted waters and o'erbear
What they are used to bear.

MENENIUS
Pray you, be gone:
I'll try whether my old wit be in request
With those that have but little: this must be patch'd
With cloth of any colour.

COMINIUS
Nay, come away.

Exeunt CORIOLANUS, COMINIUS, and others

A PATRICIAN
This man has marr'd his fortune.

MENENIUS
His nature is too noble for the world:
He would not flatter Neptune for his trident,
Or Jove for's power to thunder. His heart's his mouth:
What his breast forges, that his tongue must vent;
And, being angry, does forget that ever
He heard the name of death.

A noise within

Here's goodly work!

SECOND PATRICIAN
I would they were abed!

MENENIUS
I would they were in Tiber! What the vengeance!
Could he not speak 'em fair?

Re-enter BRUTUS and SICINIUS, with the rabble

SICINIUS
Where is this viper
That would depopulate the city and
Be every man himself?

MENENIUS
You worthy tribunes,—

SICINIUS
He shall be thrown down the Tarpeian rock
With rigorous hands: he hath resisted law,
And therefore law shall scorn him further trial
Than the severity of the public power
Which he so sets at nought.

FIRST CITIZEN

He shall well know
The noble tribunes are the people's mouths,
And we their hands.

CITIZENS
He shall, sure on't.

MENENIUS
Sir, sir,—

SICINIUS
Peace!

MENENIUS
Do not cry havoc, where you should but hunt
With modest warrant.

SICINIUS
Sir, how comes't that you
Have holp to make this rescue?

MENENIUS
Hear me speak:
As I do know the consul's worthiness,
So can I name his faults,—

SICINIUS
Consul! what consul?

MENENIUS
The consul Coriolanus.

BRUTUS
He consul!

CITIZENS
No, no, no, no, no.

MENENIUS
If, by the tribunes' leave, and yours, good people,
I may be heard, I would crave a word or two;
The which shall turn you to no further harm
Than so much loss of time.

SICINIUS
Speak briefly then;
For we are peremptory to dispatch
This viperous traitor: to eject him hence
Were but one danger, and to keep him here
Our certain death: therefore it is decreed
He dies to-night.

MENENIUS
Now the good gods forbid
That our renowned Rome, whose gratitude
Towards her deserved children is enroll'd
In Jove's own book, like an unnatural dam
Should now eat up her own!

SICINIUS
He's a disease that must be cut away.

MENENIUS
O, he's a limb that has but a disease;
Mortal, to cut it off; to cure it, easy.
What has he done to Rome that's worthy death?
Killing our enemies, the blood he hath lost—
Which, I dare vouch, is more than that he hath,
By many an ounce—he dropp'd it for his country;
And what is left, to lose it by his country,
Were to us all, that do't and suffer it,
A brand to the end o' the world.

SICINIUS
This is clean kam.

BRUTUS
Merely awry: when he did love his country,
It honour'd him.

MENENIUS
The service of the foot
Being once gangrened, is not then respected
For what before it was.

BRUTUS
We'll hear no more.
Pursue him to his house, and pluck him thence:
Lest his infection, being of catching nature,
Spread further.

MENENIUS
One word more, one word.
This tiger-footed rage, when it shall find
The harm of unscann'd swiftness, will too late
Tie leaden pounds to's heels. Proceed by process;
Lest parties, as he is beloved, break out,
And sack great Rome with Romans.

BRUTUS
If it were so,—

SICINIUS
What do ye talk?
Have we not had a taste of his obedience?
Our aediles smote? ourselves resisted? Come.

MENENIUS
Consider this: he has been bred i' the wars
Since he could draw a sword, and is ill school'd
In bolted language; meal and bran together
He throws without distinction. Give me leave,
I'll go to him, and undertake to bring him
Where he shall answer, by a lawful form,
In peace, to his utmost peril.

FIRST SENATOR
Noble tribunes,
It is the humane way: the other course
Will prove too bloody, and the end of it
Unknown to the beginning.

SICINIUS
Noble Menenius,
Be you then as the people's officer.
Masters, lay down your weapons.

BRUTUS
Go not home.

SICINIUS
Meet on the market-place. We'll attend you there:
Where, if you bring not Marcius, we'll proceed
In our first way.

MENENIUS
I'll bring him to you.

To the SENATORS

Let me desire your company: he must come,
Or what is worst will follow.

FIRST SENATOR
Pray you, let's to him.

Exeunt

SCENE II. A Room in Coriolanus's House.

Enter CORIOLANUS with PATRICIANS

CORIOLANUS
Let them puff all about mine ears, present me
Death on the wheel or at wild horses' heels,
Or pile ten hills on the Tarpeian rock,
That the precipitation might down stretch
Below the beam of sight, yet will I still
Be thus to them.

A PATRICIAN
You do the nobler.

CORIOLANUS
I muse my mother
Does not approve me further, who was wont
To call them woollen vassals, things created
To buy and sell with groats, to show bare heads
In congregations, to yawn, be still and wonder,
When one but of my ordinance stood up
To speak of peace or war.

Enter VOLUMNIA

I talk of you:
Why did you wish me milder? would you have me
False to my nature? Rather say I play
The man I am.

VOLUMNIA
O, sir, sir, sir,
I would have had you put your power well on,
Before you had worn it out.

CORIOLANUS
Let go.

VOLUMNIA
You might have been enough the man you are,
With striving less to be so; lesser had been
The thwartings of your dispositions, if
You had not show'd them how ye were disposed
Ere they lack'd power to cross you.

CORIOLANUS
Let them hang.

A Patrician
Ay, and burn too.

Enter MENENIUS and SENATORS

MENENIUS
Come, come, you have been too rough, something too rough;
You must return and mend it.

FIRST SENATOR
There's no remedy;
Unless, by not so doing, our good city
Cleave in the midst, and perish.

VOLUMNIA
Pray, be counsell'd:
I have a heart as little apt as yours,
But yet a brain that leads my use of anger
To better vantage.

MENENIUS
Well said, noble woman?
Before he should thus stoop to the herd, but that
The violent fit o' the time craves it as physic
For the whole state, I would put mine armour on,
Which I can scarcely bear.

CORIOLANUS
What must I do?

MENENIUS
Return to the tribunes.

CORIOLANUS
Well, what then? what then?

MENENIUS
Repent what you have spoke.

CORIOLANUS
For them! I cannot do it to the gods;
Must I then do't to them?

VOLUMNIA
You are too absolute;
Though therein you can never be too noble,
But when extremities speak. I have heard you say,
Honour and policy, like unsever'd friends,
I' the war do grow together: grant that, and tell me,
In peace what each of them by the other lose,
That they combine not there.

CORIOLANUS
Tush, tush!

MENENIUS
A good demand.

VOLUMNIA
If it be honour in your wars to seem
The same you are not, which, for your best ends,
You adopt your policy, how is it less or worse,
That it shall hold companionship in peace
With honour, as in war, since that to both
It stands in like request?

CORIOLANUS
Why force you this?

VOLUMNIA
Because that now it lies you on to speak
To the people; not by your own instruction,
Nor by the matter which your heart prompts you,
But with such words that are but rooted in
Your tongue, though but bastards and syllables
Of no allowance to your bosom's truth.
Now, this no more dishonours you at all
Than to take in a town with gentle words,
Which else would put you to your fortune and
The hazard of much blood.
I would dissemble with my nature where
My fortunes and my friends at stake required
I should do so in honour: I am in this,
Your wife, your son, these senators, the nobles;
And you will rather show our general louts
How you can frown than spend a fawn upon 'em,
For the inheritance of their loves and safeguard
Of what that want might ruin.

MENENIUS
Noble lady!
Come, go with us; speak fair: you may salve so,
Not what is dangerous present, but the loss
Of what is past.

VOLUMNIA
I prithee now, my son,
Go to them, with this bonnet in thy hand;
And thus far having stretch'd it—here be with them—
Thy knee bussing the stones—for in such business
Action is eloquence, and the eyes of the ignorant
More learned than the ears—waving thy head,
Which often, thus, correcting thy stout heart,
Now humble as the ripest mulberry
That will not hold the handling: or say to them,
Thou art their soldier, and being bred in broils

Hast not the soft way which, thou dost confess,
Were fit for thee to use as they to claim,
In asking their good loves, but thou wilt frame
Thyself, forsooth, hereafter theirs, so far
As thou hast power and person.

MENENIUS
This but done,
Even as she speaks, why, their hearts were yours;
For they have pardons, being ask'd, as free
As words to little purpose.

VOLUMNIA
Prithee now,
Go, and be ruled: although I know thou hadst rather
Follow thine enemy in a fiery gulf
Than flatter him in a bower. Here is Cominius.

Enter COMINIUS

COMINIUS
I have been i' the market-place; and, sir,'tis fit
You make strong party, or defend yourself
By calmness or by absence: all's in anger.

MENENIUS
Only fair speech.

COMINIUS
I think 'twill serve, if he
Can thereto frame his spirit.

VOLUMNIA
He must, and will
Prithee now, say you will, and go about it.

CORIOLANUS
Must I go show them my unbarbed sconce?
Must I with base tongue give my noble heart
A lie that it must bear? Well, I will do't:
Yet, were there but this single plot to lose,
This mould of Marcius, they to dust should grind it
And throw't against the wind. To the market-place!
You have put me now to such a part which never
I shall discharge to the life.

COMINIUS
Come, come, we'll prompt you.

VOLUMNIA

I prithee now, sweet son, as thou hast said
My praises made thee first a soldier, so,
To have my praise for this, perform a part
Thou hast not done before.

CORIOLANUS
Well, I must do't:
Away, my disposition, and possess me
Some harlot's spirit! my throat of war be turn'd,
Which quired with my drum, into a pipe
Small as an eunuch, or the virgin voice
That babies lulls asleep! the smiles of knaves
Tent in my cheeks, and schoolboys' tears take up
The glasses of my sight! a beggar's tongue
Make motion through my lips, and my arm'd knees,
Who bow'd but in my stirrup, bend like his
That hath received an alms! I will not do't,
Lest I surcease to honour mine own truth
And by my body's action teach my mind
A most inherent baseness.

VOLUMNIA
At thy choice, then:
To beg of thee, it is my more dishonour
Than thou of them. Come all to ruin; let
Thy mother rather feel thy pride than fear
Thy dangerous stoutness, for I mock at death
With as big heart as thou. Do as thou list
Thy valiantness was mine, thou suck'dst it from me,
But owe thy pride thyself.

CORIOLANUS
Pray, be content:
Mother, I am going to the market-place;
Chide me no more. I'll mountebank their loves,
Cog their hearts from them, and come home beloved
Of all the trades in Rome. Look, I am going:
Commend me to my wife. I'll return consul;
Or never trust to what my tongue can do
I' the way of flattery further.

VOLUMNIA
Do your will.

Exit

COMINIUS
Away! the tribunes do attend you: arm yourself
To answer mildly; for they are prepared
With accusations, as I hear, more strong
Than are upon you yet.

CORIOLANUS
The word is 'mildly.' Pray you, let us go:
Let them accuse me by invention, I
Will answer in mine honour.

MENENIUS
Ay, but mildly.

CORIOLANUS
Well, mildly be it then. Mildly!

Exeunt

SCENE III. The Same. The Forum.

Enter SICINIUS and BRUTUS

BRUTUS
In this point charge him home, that he affects
Tyrannical power: if he evade us there,
Enforce him with his envy to the people,
And that the spoil got on the Antiates
Was ne'er distributed.

Enter an AEDILE

What, will he come?

AEDILE
He's coming.

BRUTUS
How accompanied?

AEDILE
With old Menenius, and those senators
That always favour'd him.

SICINIUS
Have you a catalogue
Of all the voices that we have procured
Set down by the poll?

AEDILE
I have; 'tis ready.

SICINIUS
Have you collected them by tribes?

AEDILE
I have.

SICINIUS
Assemble presently the people hither;
And when they bear me say 'It shall be so
I' the right and strength o' the commons,' be it either
For death, for fine, or banishment, then let them
If I say fine, cry 'Fine;' if death, cry 'Death.'
Insisting on the old prerogative
And power i' the truth o' the cause.

AEDILE
I shall inform them.

BRUTUS
And when such time they have begun to cry,
Let them not cease, but with a din confused
Enforce the present execution
Of what we chance to sentence.

AEDILE
Very well.

SICINIUS
Make them be strong and ready for this hint,
When we shall hap to give 't them.

BRUTUS
Go about it.

Exit AEDILE

Put him to choler straight: he hath been used
Ever to conquer, and to have his worth
Of contradiction: being once chafed, he cannot
Be rein'd again to temperance; then he speaks
What's in his heart; and that is there which looks
With us to break his neck.

SICINIUS
Well, here he comes.

Enter CORIOLANUS, MENENIUS, and COMINIUS, with SENATORS and PATRICIANS

MENENIUS
Calmly, I do beseech you.

CORIOLANUS

Ay, as an ostler, that for the poorest piece
Will bear the knave by the volume. The honour'd gods
Keep Rome in safety, and the chairs of justice
Supplied with worthy men! plant love among 's!
Throng our large temples with the shows of peace,
And not our streets with war!

FIRST SENATOR
Amen, amen.

MENENIUS
A noble wish.

Re-enter AEDILE, with CITIZENS

SICINIUS
Draw near, ye people.

AEDILE
List to your tribunes. Audience: peace, I say!

CORIOLANUS
First, hear me speak.

BOTH TRIBUNES
Well, say. Peace, ho!

CORIOLANUS
Shall I be charged no further than this present?
Must all determine here?

SICINIUS
I do demand,
If you submit you to the people's voices,
Allow their officers and are content
To suffer lawful censure for such faults
As shall be proved upon you?

CORIOLANUS
I am content.

MENENIUS
Lo, citizens, he says he is content:
The warlike service he has done, consider; think
Upon the wounds his body bears, which show
Like graves i' the holy churchyard.

CORIOLANUS
Scratches with briers,
Scars to move laughter only.

MENENIUS
Consider further,
That when he speaks not like a citizen,
You find him like a soldier: do not take
His rougher accents for malicious sounds,
But, as I say, such as become a soldier,
Rather than envy you.

COMINIUS
Well, well, no more.

CORIOLANUS
What is the matter
That being pass'd for consul with full voice,
I am so dishonour'd that the very hour
You take it off again?

SICINIUS
Answer to us.

CORIOLANUS
Say, then: 'tis true, I ought so.

SICINIUS
We charge you, that you have contrived to take
From Rome all season'd office and to wind
Yourself into a power tyrannical;
For which you are a traitor to the people.

CORIOLANUS
How! traitor!

MENENIUS
Nay, temperately; your promise.

CORIOLANUS
The fires i' the lowest hell fold-in the people!
Call me their traitor! Thou injurious tribune!
Within thine eyes sat twenty thousand deaths,
In thy hand clutch'd as many millions, in
Thy lying tongue both numbers, I would say
'Thou liest' unto thee with a voice as free
As I do pray the gods.

SICINIUS
Mark you this, people?

CITIZENS
To the rock, to the rock with him!

SICINIUS

Peace!
We need not put new matter to his charge:
What you have seen him do and heard him speak,
Beating your officers, cursing yourselves,
Opposing laws with strokes and here defying
Those whose great power must try him; even this,
So criminal and in such capital kind,
Deserves the extremest death.

BRUTUS
But since he hath
Served well for Rome,—

CORIOLANUS
What do you prate of service?

BRUTUS
I talk of that, that know it.

CORIOLANUS
You?

MENENIUS
Is this the promise that you made your mother?

COMINIUS
Know, I pray you,—

CORIOLANUS
I know no further:
Let them pronounce the steep Tarpeian death,
Vagabond exile, raying, pent to linger
But with a grain a day, I would not buy
Their mercy at the price of one fair word;
Nor cheque my courage for what they can give,
To have't with saying 'Good morrow.'

SICINIUS
For that he has,
As much as in him lies, from time to time
Envied against the people, seeking means
To pluck away their power, as now at last
Given hostile strokes, and that not in the presence
Of dreaded justice, but on the ministers
That do distribute it; in the name o' the people
And in the power of us the tribunes, we,
Even from this instant, banish him our city,
In peril of precipitation
From off the rock Tarpeian never more
To enter our Rome gates: i' the people's name,
I say it shall be so.

CITIZENS
It shall be so, it shall be so; let him away:
He's banish'd, and it shall be so.

COMINIUS
Hear me, my masters, and my common friends,—

SICINIUS
He's sentenced; no more hearing.

COMINIUS
Let me speak:
I have been consul, and can show for Rome
Her enemies' marks upon me. I do love
My country's good with a respect more tender,
More holy and profound, than mine own life,
My dear wife's estimate, her womb's increase,
And treasure of my loins; then if I would
Speak that,—

SICINIUS
We know your drift: speak what?

BRUTUS
There's no more to be said, but he is banish'd,
As enemy to the people and his country:
It shall be so.

CITIZENS
It shall be so, it shall be so.

CORIOLANUS
You common cry of curs! whose breath I hate
As reek o' the rotten fens, whose loves I prize
As the dead carcasses of unburied men
That do corrupt my air, I banish you;
And here remain with your uncertainty!
Let every feeble rumour shake your hearts!
Your enemies, with nodding of their plumes,
Fan you into despair! Have the power still
To banish your defenders; till at length
Your ignorance, which finds not till it feels,
Making not reservation of yourselves,
Still your own foes, deliver you as most
Abated captives to some nation
That won you without blows! Despising,
For you, the city, thus I turn my back:
There is a world elsewhere.

Exeunt CORIOLANUS, COMINIUS, MENENIUS, SENATORS, and PATRICIANS

AEDILE
The people's enemy is gone, is gone!

CITIZENS
Our enemy is banish'd! he is gone! Hoo! hoo!

Shouting, and throwing up their caps

SICINIUS
Go, see him out at gates, and follow him,
As he hath followed you, with all despite;
Give him deserved vexation. Let a guard
Attend us through the city.

CITIZENS
Come, come; let's see him out at gates; come.
The gods preserve our noble tribunes! Come.

Exeunt

ACT IV

SCENE I. Rome. Before a Gate of the City.

Enter CORIOLANUS, VOLUMNIA, VIRGILIA, MENENIUS, COMINIUS, with the young Nobility of Rome

CORIOLANUS
Come, leave your tears: a brief farewell: the beast
With many heads butts me away. Nay, mother,
Where is your ancient courage? you were used
To say extremity was the trier of spirits;
That common chances common men could bear;
That when the sea was calm all boats alike
Show'd mastership in floating; fortune's blows,
When most struck home, being gentle wounded, craves
A noble cunning: you were used to load me
With precepts that would make invincible
The heart that conn'd them.

VIRGILIA
O heavens! O heavens!

CORIOLANUS
Nay! prithee, woman,—

VOLUMNIA

Now the red pestilence strike all trades in Rome,
And occupations perish!

CORIOLANUS
What, what, what!
I shall be loved when I am lack'd. Nay, mother.
Resume that spirit, when you were wont to say,
If you had been the wife of Hercules,
Six of his labours you'ld have done, and saved
Your husband so much sweat. Cominius,
Droop not; adieu. Farewell, my wife, my mother:
I'll do well yet. Thou old and true Menenius,
Thy tears are salter than a younger man's,
And venomous to thine eyes. My sometime general,
I have seen thee stem, and thou hast oft beheld
Heart-hardening spectacles; tell these sad women
'Tis fond to wail inevitable strokes,
As 'tis to laugh at 'em. My mother, you wot well
My hazards still have been your solace: and
Believe't not lightly—though I go alone,
Like to a lonely dragon, that his fen
Makes fear'd and talk'd of more than seen—your son
Will or exceed the common or be caught
With cautelous baits and practise.

VOLUMNIA
My first son.
Whither wilt thou go? Take good Cominius
With thee awhile: determine on some course,
More than a wild exposture to each chance
That starts i' the way before thee.

CORIOLANUS
O the gods!

COMINIUS
I'll follow thee a month, devise with thee
Where thou shalt rest, that thou mayst hear of us
And we of thee: so if the time thrust forth
A cause for thy repeal, we shall not send
O'er the vast world to seek a single man,
And lose advantage, which doth ever cool
I' the absence of the needer.

CORIOLANUS
Fare ye well:
Thou hast years upon thee; and thou art too full
Of the wars' surfeits, to go rove with one
That's yet unbruised: bring me but out at gate.
Come, my sweet wife, my dearest mother, and
My friends of noble touch, when I am forth,

Bid me farewell, and smile. I pray you, come.
While I remain above the ground, you shall
Hear from me still, and never of me aught
But what is like me formerly.

MENENIUS
That's worthily
As any ear can hear. Come, let's not weep.
If I could shake off but one seven years
From these old arms and legs, by the good gods,
I'ld with thee every foot.

CORIOLANUS
Give me thy hand: Come.

Exeunt

SCENE II. The Same. A Street Near the Gate.

Enter SICINIUS, BRUTUS, and an AEDILE

SICINIUS
Bid them all home; he's gone, and we'll no further.
The nobility are vex'd, whom we see have sided
In his behalf.

BRUTUS
Now we have shown our power,
Let us seem humbler after it is done
Than when it was a-doing.

SICINIUS
Bid them home:
Say their great enemy is gone, and they
Stand in their ancient strength.

BRUTUS
Dismiss them home.

Exit AEDILE

Here comes his mother.

SICINIUS
Let's not meet her.

BRUTUS
Why?

SICINIUS
They say she's mad.

BRUTUS
They have ta'en note of us: keep on your way.

Enter VOLUMNIA, VIRGILIA, and MENENIUS

VOLUMNIA
O, ye're well met: the hoarded plague o' the gods
Requite your love!

MENENIUS
Peace, peace; be not so loud.

VOLUMNIA
If that I could for weeping, you should hear,—
Nay, and you shall hear some.

To BRUTUS

Will you be gone?

VIRGILIA
[To SICINIUS] You shall stay too: I would I had the power
To say so to my husband.

SICINIUS
Are you mankind?

VOLUMNIA
Ay, fool; is that a shame? Note but this fool.
Was not a man my father? Hadst thou foxship
To banish him that struck more blows for Rome
Than thou hast spoken words?

SICINIUS
O blessed heavens!

VOLUMNIA
More noble blows than ever thou wise words;
And for Rome's good. I'll tell thee what; yet go:
Nay, but thou shalt stay too: I would my son
Were in Arabia, and thy tribe before him,
His good sword in his hand.

SICINIUS
What then?

VIRGILIA

What then!
He'ld make an end of thy posterity.

VOLUMNIA
Bastards and all.
Good man, the wounds that he does bear for Rome!

MENENIUS
Come, come, peace.

SICINIUS
I would he had continued to his country
As he began, and not unknit himself
The noble knot he made.

BRUTUS
I would he had.

VOLUMNIA
'I would he had'! 'Twas you incensed the rabble:
Cats, that can judge as fitly of his worth
As I can of those mysteries which heaven
Will not have earth to know.

BRUTUS
Pray, let us go.

VOLUMNIA
Now, pray, sir, get you gone:
You have done a brave deed. Ere you go, hear this:—
As far as doth the Capitol exceed
The meanest house in Rome, so far my son—
This lady's husband here, this, do you see—
Whom you have banish'd, does exceed you all.

BRUTUS
Well, well, we'll leave you.

SICINIUS
Why stay we to be baited
With one that wants her wits?

VOLUMNIA
Take my prayers with you.

Exeunt TRIBUNES

I would the gods had nothing else to do
But to confirm my curses! Could I meet 'em
But once a-day, it would unclog my heart
Of what lies heavy to't.

MENENIUS
You have told them home;
And, by my troth, you have cause. You'll sup with me?

VOLUMNIA
Anger's my meat; I sup upon myself,
And so shall starve with feeding. Come, let's go:
Leave this faint puling and lament as I do,
In anger, Juno-like. Come, come, come.

MENENIUS
Fie, fie, fie!

Exeunt

SCENE III. A Highway Between Rome and Antium.

Enter a ROMAN and a VOLSCE, meeting

ROMAN
I know you well, sir, and you know me: your name, I think, is Adrian.

VOLSCE
It is so, sir: truly, I have forgot you.

ROMAN
I am a Roman; and my services are, as you are, against 'em: know you me yet?

VOLSCE
Nicanor? no.

ROMAN
The same, sir.

VOLSCE
You had more beard when I last saw you; but your favour is well approved by your tongue. What's the news in Rome? I have a note from the Volscian state, to find you out there: you have well saved me a day's journey.

ROMAN
There hath been in Rome strange insurrections; the people against the senators, patricians, and nobles.

VOLSCE
Hath been! is it ended, then? Our state thinks not so: they are in a most warlike preparation, and hope to come upon them in the heat of their division.

ROMAN

The main blaze of it is past, but a small thing would make it flame again: for the nobles receive so to heart the banishment of that worthy Coriolanus, that they are in a ripe aptness to take all power from the people and to pluck from them their tribunes for ever. This lies glowing, I can tell you, and is almost mature for the violent breaking out.

VOLSCE
Coriolanus banished!

ROMAN
Banished, sir.

VOLSCE
You will be welcome with this intelligence, Nicanor.

ROMAN
The day serves well for them now. I have heard it said, the fittest time to corrupt a man's wife is when she's fallen out with her husband. Your noble Tullus Aufidius will appear well in these wars, his great opposer, Coriolanus, being now in no request of his country.

VOLSCE
He cannot choose. I am most fortunate, thus accidentally to encounter you: you have ended my business, and I will merrily accompany you home.

ROMAN
I shall, between this and supper, tell you most strange things from Rome; all tending to the good of their adversaries. Have you an army ready, say you?

VOLSCE
A most royal one; the centurions and their charges, distinctly billeted, already in the entertainment, and to be on foot at an hour's warning.

ROMAN
I am joyful to hear of their readiness, and am the man, I think, that shall set them in present action. So, sir, heartily well met, and most glad of your company.

VOLSCE
You take my part from me, sir; I have the most cause to be glad of yours.

ROMAN
Well, let us go together.

Exeunt

SCENE IV. Antium. Before Aufidius's House.

Enter CORIOLANUS in mean apparel, disguised and muffled

CORIOLANUS
A goodly city is this Antium. City,
'Tis I that made thy widows: many an heir

Of these fair edifices 'fore my wars
Have I heard groan and drop: then know me not,
Lest that thy wives with spits and boys with stones
In puny battle slay me.

Enter a CITIZEN

Save you, sir.

CITIZEN
And you.

CORIOLANUS
Direct me, if it be your will,
Where great Aufidius lies: is he in Antium?

CITIZEN
He is, and feasts the nobles of the state
At his house this night.

CORIOLANUS
Which is his house, beseech you?

CITIZEN
This, here before you.

CORIOLANUS
Thank you, sir: farewell.

Exit CITIZEN

O world, thy slippery turns! Friends now fast sworn,
Whose double bosoms seem to wear one heart,
Whose house, whose bed, whose meal, and exercise,
Are still together, who twin, as 'twere, in love
Unseparable, shall within this hour,
On a dissension of a doit, break out
To bitterest enmity: so, fellest foes,
Whose passions and whose plots have broke their sleep,
To take the one the other, by some chance,
Some trick not worth an egg, shall grow dear friends
And interjoin their issues. So with me:
My birth-place hate I, and my love's upon
This enemy town. I'll enter: if he slay me,
He does fair justice; if he give me way,
I'll do his country service.

Exit

SCENE V. The Same. A Hall in Aufidius's House.

Music within. Enter a SERVINGMAN

FIRST SERVINGMAN
Wine, wine, wine! What service is here! I think our fellows are asleep.

Exit

Enter a SECOND SERVINGMAN

SECOND SERVINGMAN
Where's Cotus? my master calls for him. Cotus!

Exit

Enter CORIOLANUS

CORIOLANUS
A goodly house: the feast smells well; but I
Appear not like a guest.

Re-enter the FIRST SERVINGMAN

FIRST SERVINGMAN
What would you have, friend? whence are you?
Here's no place for you: pray, go to the door.

Exit

CORIOLANUS
I have deserved no better entertainment,
In being Coriolanus.

Re-enter SECOND SERVINGMAN

SECOND SERVINGMAN
Whence are you, sir? Has the porter his eyes in his head; that he gives entrance to such companions? Pray, get you out.

CORIOLANUS
Away!

SECOND SERVINGMAN
Away! get you away.

CORIOLANUS
Now thou'rt troublesome.

SECOND SERVINGMAN
Are you so brave? I'll have you talked with anon.

Enter a THIRD SERVINGMAN. The FIRST meets him

THIRD SERVINGMAN
What fellow's this?

FIRST SERVINGMAN
A strange one as ever I looked on: I cannot get him out of the house: prithee, call my master to him.

Retires

THIRD SERVINGMAN
What have you to do here, fellow? Pray you, avoid the house.

CORIOLANUS
Let me but stand; I will not hurt your hearth.

THIRD SERVINGMAN
What are you?

CORIOLANUS
A gentleman.

THIRD SERVINGMAN
A marvellous poor one.

CORIOLANUS
True, so I am.

THIRD SERVINGMAN
Pray you, poor gentleman, take up some other station; here's no place for you; pray you, avoid: come.

CORIOLANUS
Follow your function, go, and batten on cold bits.

Pushes him away

THIRD SERVINGMAN
What, you will not? Prithee, tell my master what a strange guest he has here.

SECOND SERVINGMAN
And I shall.

Exit

THIRD SERVINGMAN
Where dwellest thou?

CORIOLANUS
Under the canopy.

THIRD SERVINGMAN
Under the canopy!

CORIOLANUS
Ay.

THIRD SERVINGMAN
Where's that?

CORIOLANUS
I' the city of kites and crows.

THIRD SERVINGMAN
I' the city of kites and crows! What an ass it is!
Then thou dwellest with daws too?

CORIOLANUS
No, I serve not thy master.

THIRD SERVINGMAN
How, sir! do you meddle with my master?

CORIOLANUS
Ay; 'tis an honester service than to meddle with thy mistress. Thou pratest, and pratest; serve with thy trencher, hence!

Beats him away.

Exit THIRD SERVINGMAN

Enter AUFIDIUS with the SECOND SERVINGMAN

AUFIDIUS
Where is this fellow?

SECOND SERVINGMAN
Here, sir: I'd have beaten him like a dog, but for disturbing the lords within.

Retires

AUFIDIUS
Whence comest thou? what wouldst thou? thy name?
Why speak'st not? speak, man: what's thy name?

CORIOLANUS
If, Tullus,

Unmuffling

Not yet thou knowest me, and, seeing me, dost not
Think me for the man I am, necessity
Commands me name myself.

AUFIDIUS
What is thy name?

CORIOLANUS
A name unmusical to the Volscians' ears,
And harsh in sound to thine.

AUFIDIUS
Say, what's thy name?
Thou hast a grim appearance, and thy face
Bears a command in't; though thy tackle's torn.
Thou show'st a noble vessel: what's thy name?

CORIOLANUS
Prepare thy brow to frown: know'st
thou me yet?

AUFIDIUS
I know thee not: thy name?

CORIOLANUS
My name is Caius Marcius, who hath done
To thee particularly and to all the Volsces
Great hurt and mischief; thereto witness may
My surname, Coriolanus: the painful service,
The extreme dangers and the drops of blood
Shed for my thankless country are requited
But with that surname; a good memory,
And witness of the malice and displeasure
Which thou shouldst bear me: only that name remains;
The cruelty and envy of the people,
Permitted by our dastard nobles, who
Have all forsook me, hath devour'd the rest;
And suffer'd me by the voice of slaves to be
Whoop'd out of Rome. Now this extremity
Hath brought me to thy hearth; not out of hope—
Mistake me not—to save my life, for if
I had fear'd death, of all the men i' the world
I would have 'voided thee, but in mere spite,
To be full quit of those my banishers,
Stand I before thee here. Then if thou hast
A heart of wreak in thee, that wilt revenge
Thine own particular wrongs and stop those maims
Of shame seen through thy country, speed thee straight,
And make my misery serve thy turn: so use it
That my revengeful services may prove
As benefits to thee, for I will fight

Against my canker'd country with the spleen
Of all the under fiends. But if so be
Thou darest not this and that to prove more fortunes
Thou'rt tired, then, in a word, I also am
Longer to live most weary, and present
My throat to thee and to thy ancient malice;
Which not to cut would show thee but a fool,
Since I have ever follow'd thee with hate,
Drawn tuns of blood out of thy country's breast,
And cannot live but to thy shame, unless
It be to do thee service.

AUFIDIUS
O Marcius, Marcius!
Each word thou hast spoke hath weeded from my heart
A root of ancient envy. If Jupiter
Should from yond cloud speak divine things,
And say 'Tis true,' I'd not believe them more
Than thee, all noble Marcius. Let me twine
Mine arms about that body, where against
My grained ash an hundred times hath broke
And scarr'd the moon with splinters: here I clip
The anvil of my sword, and do contest
As hotly and as nobly with thy love
As ever in ambitious strength I did
Contend against thy valour. Know thou first,
I loved the maid I married; never man
Sigh'd truer breath; but that I see thee here,
Thou noble thing! more dances my rapt heart
Than when I first my wedded mistress saw
Bestride my threshold. Why, thou Mars! I tell thee,
We have a power on foot; and I had purpose
Once more to hew thy target from thy brawn,
Or lose mine arm fort: thou hast beat me out
Twelve several times, and I have nightly since
Dreamt of encounters 'twixt thyself and me;
We have been down together in my sleep,
Unbuckling helms, fisting each other's throat,
And waked half dead with nothing. Worthy Marcius,
Had we no quarrel else to Rome, but that
Thou art thence banish'd, we would muster all
From twelve to seventy, and pouring war
Into the bowels of ungrateful Rome,
Like a bold flood o'er-bear. O, come, go in,
And take our friendly senators by the hands;
Who now are here, taking their leaves of me,
Who am prepared against your territories,
Though not for Rome itself.

CORIOLANUS
You bless me, gods!

AUFIDIUS
Therefore, most absolute sir, if thou wilt have
The leading of thine own revenges, take
The one half of my commission; and set down—
As best thou art experienced, since thou know'st
Thy country's strength and weakness,—thine own ways;
Whether to knock against the gates of Rome,
Or rudely visit them in parts remote,
To fright them, ere destroy. But come in:
Let me commend thee first to those that shall
Say yea to thy desires. A thousand welcomes!
And more a friend than e'er an enemy;
Yet, Marcius, that was much. Your hand: most welcome!

Exeunt CORIOLANUS and AUFIDIUS.

The TWO SERVINGMEN come forward

FIRST SERVINGMAN
Here's a strange alteration!

SECOND SERVINGMAN
By my hand, I had thought to have strucken him with a cudgel; and yet my mind gave me his clothes made a false report of him.

FIRST SERVINGMAN
What an arm he has! he turned me about with his finger and his thumb, as one would set up a top.

SECOND SERVINGMAN
Nay, I knew by his face that there was something in him: he had, sir, a kind of face, methought,—I cannot tell how to term it.

FIRST SERVINGMAN
He had so; looking as it were—would I were hanged, but I thought there was more in him than I could think.

SECOND SERVINGMAN
So did I, I'll be sworn: he is simply the rarest man i' the world.

FIRST SERVINGMAN
I think he is: but a greater soldier than he you wot on.

SECOND SERVINGMAN
Who, my master?

FIRST SERVINGMAN
Nay, it's no matter for that.

SECOND SERVINGMAN
Worth six on him.

FIRST SERVINGMAN
Nay, not so neither: but I take him to be the greater soldier.

SECOND SERVINGMAN
Faith, look you, one cannot tell how to say that: for the defence of a town, our general is excellent.

FIRST SERVINGMAN
Ay, and for an assault too.

Re-enter THIRD SERVINGMAN

THIRD SERVINGMAN
O slaves, I can tell you news,— news, you rascals!

FIRST SERVINGMAN/SECOND SERVINGMAN
What, what, what? let's partake.

THIRD SERVINGMAN
I would not be a Roman, of all nations; I had as lieve be a condemned man.

FIRST SERVINGMAN/SECOND SERVINGMAN
Wherefore? wherefore?

THIRD SERVINGMAN
Why, here's he that was wont to thwack our general, Caius Marcius.

FIRST SERVINGMAN
Why do you say 'thwack our general'?

FIRST SERVINGMAN
I do not say 'thwack our general;' but he was always good enough for him.

SECOND SERVINGMAN
Come, we are fellows and friends: he was ever too hard for him; I have heard him say so himself.

FIRST SERVINGMAN
He was too hard for him directly, to say the troth on't: before Corioli he scotched him and notched him like a carbonado.

SECOND SERVINGMAN
An he had been cannibally given, he might have broiled and eaten him too.

FIRST SERVINGMAN
But, more of thy news?

THIRD SERVINGMAN
Why, he is so made on here within, as if he were son and heir to Mars; set at upper end o' the table; no question asked him by any of the senators, but they stand bald before him: our general himself makes a mistress of him: sanctifies himself with's hand and turns up the white o' the eye to his discourse. But the bottom of the news is that our general is cut i' the middle and but one half of

what he was yesterday; for the other has half, by the entreaty and grant of the whole table. He'll go, he says, and sowl the porter of Rome gates by the ears: he will mow all down before him, and leave his passage polled.

SECOND SERVINGMAN
And he's as like to do't as any man I can imagine.

THIRD SERVINGMAN
Do't! he will do't; for, look you, sir, he has as many friends as enemies; which friends, sir, as it were, durst not, look you, sir, show themselves, as we term it, his friends whilst he's in directitude.

FIRST SERVINGMAN
Directitude! what's that?

THIRD SERVINGMAN
But when they shall see, sir, his crest up again, and the man in blood, they will out of their burrows, like conies after rain, and revel all with him.

FIRST SERVINGMAN
But when goes this forward?

THIRD SERVINGMAN
To-morrow; to-day; presently; you shall have the drum struck up this afternoon: 'tis, as it were, a parcel of their feast, and to be executed ere they wipe their lips.

SECOND SERVINGMAN
Why, then we shall have a stirring world again. This peace is nothing, but to rust iron, increase tailors, and breed ballad-makers.

FIRST SERVINGMAN
Let me have war, say I; it exceeds peace as far as day does night; it's spritely, waking, audible, and full of vent. Peace is a very apoplexy, lethargy; mulled, deaf, sleepy, insensible; a getter of more bastard children than war's a destroyer of men.

SECOND SERVINGMAN
'Tis so: and as war, in some sort, may be said to be a ravisher, so it cannot be denied but peace is a great maker of cuckolds.

FIRST SERVINGMAN
Ay, and it makes men hate one another.

THIRD SERVINGMAN
Reason; because they then less need one another. The wars for my money. I hope to see Romans as cheap as Volscians. They are rising, they are rising.

ALL
In, in, in, in!

Exeunt

SCENE VI. Rome. A Public Place.

Enter SICINIUS and BRUTUS

SICINIUS
We hear not of him, neither need we fear him;
His remedies are tame i' the present peace
And quietness of the people, which before
Were in wild hurry. Here do we make his friends
Blush that the world goes well, who rather had,
Though they themselves did suffer by't, behold
Dissentious numbers pestering streets than see
Our tradesmen with in their shops and going
About their functions friendly.

BRUTUS
We stood to't in good time.

Enter MENENIUS

Is this Menenius?

SICINIUS
'Tis he,'tis he: O, he is grown most kind of late.

Both Tribunes
Hail sir!

MENENIUS
Hail to you both!

SICINIUS
Your Coriolanus
Is not much miss'd, but with his friends:
The commonwealth doth stand, and so would do,
Were he more angry at it.

MENENIUS
All's well; and might have been much better, if
He could have temporized.

SICINIUS
Where is he, hear you?

MENENIUS
Nay, I hear nothing: his mother and his wife
Hear nothing from him.

Enter three or four CITIZENS

CITIZENS

The gods preserve you both!

SICINIUS
God-den, our neighbours.

BRUTUS
God-den to you all, god-den to you all.

FIRST CITIZEN
Ourselves, our wives, and children, on our knees,
Are bound to pray for you both.

SICINIUS
Live, and thrive!

BRUTUS
Farewell, kind neighbours: we wish'd Coriolanus
Had loved you as we did.

CITIZENS
Now the gods keep you!

BOTH TRIBUNES
Farewell, farewell.

Exeunt CITIZENS

SICINIUS
This is a happier and more comely time
Than when these fellows ran about the streets,
Crying confusion.

BRUTUS
Caius Marcius was
A worthy officer i' the war; but insolent,
O'ercome with pride, ambitious past all thinking,
Self-loving,—

SICINIUS
And affecting one sole throne,
Without assistance.

MENENIUS
I think not so.

SICINIUS
We should by this, to all our lamentation,
If he had gone forth consul, found it so.

BRUTUS

The gods have well prevented it, and Rome
Sits safe and still without him.

Enter an AEDILE

AEDILE
Worthy tribunes,
There is a slave, whom we have put in prison,
Reports, the Volsces with two several powers
Are enter'd in the Roman territories,
And with the deepest malice of the war
Destroy what lies before 'em.

MENENIUS
'Tis Aufidius,
Who, hearing of our Marcius' banishment,
Thrusts forth his horns again into the world;
Which were inshell'd when Marcius stood for Rome,
And durst not once peep out.

SICINIUS
Come, what talk you
Of Marcius?

BRUTUS
Go see this rumourer whipp'd. It cannot be
The Volsces dare break with us.

MENENIUS
Cannot be!
We have record that very well it can,
And three examples of the like have been
Within my age. But reason with the fellow,
Before you punish him, where he heard this,
Lest you shall chance to whip your information
And beat the messenger who bids beware
Of what is to be dreaded.

SICINIUS
Tell not me:
I know this cannot be.

BRUTUS
Not possible.

Enter a MESSENGER

MESSENGER
The nobles in great earnestness are going
All to the senate-house: some news is come
That turns their countenances.

SICINIUS
'Tis this slave;—
Go whip him, 'fore the people's eyes:—his raising;
Nothing but his report.

MESSENGER
Yes, worthy sir,
The slave's report is seconded; and more,
More fearful, is deliver'd.

SICINIUS
What more fearful?

MESSENGER
It is spoke freely out of many mouths—
How probable I do not know—that Marcius,
Join'd with Aufidius, leads a power 'gainst Rome,
And vows revenge as spacious as between
The young'st and oldest thing.

SICINIUS
This is most likely!

BRUTUS
Raised only, that the weaker sort may wish
Good Marcius home again.

SICINIUS
The very trick on't.

MENENIUS
This is unlikely:
He and Aufidius can no more atone
Than violentest contrariety.

Enter a SECOND MESSENGER

SECOND MESSENGER
You are sent for to the senate:
A fearful army, led by Caius Marcius
Associated with Aufidius, rages
Upon our territories; and have already
O'erborne their way, consumed with fire, and took
What lay before them.

Enter COMINIUS

COMINIUS
O, you have made good work!

MENENIUS
What news? what news?

COMINIUS
You have holp to ravish your own daughters and
To melt the city leads upon your pates,
To see your wives dishonour'd to your noses,—

MENENIUS
What's the news? what's the news?

COMINIUS
Your temples burned in their cement, and
Your franchises, whereon you stood, confined
Into an auger's bore.

MENENIUS
Pray now, your news?
You have made fair work, I fear me.—Pray, your news?—
If Marcius should be join'd with Volscians,—

COMINIUS
If! He is their god: he leads them like a thing
Made by some other deity than nature,
That shapes man better; and they follow him,
Against us brats, with no less confidence
Than boys pursuing summer butterflies,
Or butchers killing flies.

MENENIUS
You have made good work,
You and your apron-men; you that stood so up much
on the voice of occupation and
The breath of garlic-eaters!

COMINIUS
He will shake
Your Rome about your ears.

MENENIUS
As Hercules
Did shake down mellow fruit.
You have made fair work!

BRUTUS
But is this true, sir?

COMINIUS
Ay; and you'll look pale
Before you find it other. All the regions
Do smilingly revolt; and who resist

Are mock'd for valiant ignorance,
And perish constant fools. Who is't can blame him?
Your enemies and his find something in him.

MENENIUS
We are all undone, unless
The noble man have mercy.

COMINIUS
Who shall ask it?
The tribunes cannot do't for shame; the people
Deserve such pity of him as the wolf
Does of the shepherds: for his best friends, if they
Should say 'Be good to Rome,' they charged him even
As those should do that had deserved his hate,
And therein show'd like enemies.

MENENIUS
'Tis true:
If he were putting to my house the brand
That should consume it, I have not the face
To say 'Beseech you, cease.' You have made fair hands,
You and your crafts! you have crafted fair!

COMINIUS
You have brought
A trembling upon Rome, such as was never
So incapable of help.

BOTH TRIBUNES
Say not we brought it.

MENENIUS
How! Was it we? we loved him but, like beasts
And cowardly nobles, gave way unto your clusters,
Who did hoot him out o' the city.

COMINIUS
But I fear
They'll roar him in again. Tullus Aufidius,
The second name of men, obeys his points
As if he were his officer: desperation
Is all the policy, strength and defence,
That Rome can make against them.

Enter a troop of CITIZENS

MENENIUS
Here come the clusters.
And is Aufidius with him? You are they
That made the air unwholesome, when you cast

Your stinking greasy caps in hooting at
Coriolanus' exile. Now he's coming;
And not a hair upon a soldier's head
Which will not prove a whip: as many coxcombs
As you threw caps up will he tumble down,
And pay you for your voices. 'Tis no matter;
if he could burn us all into one coal,
We have deserved it.

CITIZENS
Faith, we hear fearful news.

FIRST CITIZEN
For mine own part,
When I said, banish him, I said 'twas pity.

SECOND CITIZEN
And so did I.

THIRD CITIZEN
And so did I; and, to say the truth, so did very many of us: that we did, we did for the best; and though we willingly consented to his banishment, yet it was against our will.

COMINIUS
Ye re goodly things, you voices!

MENENIUS
You have made
Good work, you and your cry! Shall's to the Capitol?

COMINIUS
O, ay, what else?

Exeunt COMINIUS and MENENIUS

SICINIUS
Go, masters, get you home; be not dismay'd:
These are a side that would be glad to have
This true which they so seem to fear. Go home,
And show no sign of fear.

FIRST CITIZEN
The gods be good to us! Come, masters, let's home.
I ever said we were i' the wrong when we banished him.

SECOND CITIZEN
So did we all. But, come, let's home.

Exeunt CITIZENS

BRUTUS

I do not like this news.

SICINIUS
Nor I.

BRUTUS
Let's to the Capitol. Would half my wealth
Would buy this for a lie!

SICINIUS
Pray, let us go.

Exeunt

SCENE VII. A Camp, at a Small Distance from Rome.

Enter AUFIDIUS and his LIEUTENANT

AUFIDIUS
Do they still fly to the Roman?

LIEUTENANT
I do not know what witchcraft's in him, but
Your soldiers use him as the grace 'fore meat,
Their talk at table, and their thanks at end;
And you are darken'd in this action, sir,
Even by your own.

AUFIDIUS
I cannot help it now,
Unless, by using means, I lame the foot
Of our design. He bears himself more proudlier,
Even to my person, than I thought he would
When first I did embrace him: yet his nature
In that's no changeling; and I must excuse
What cannot be amended.

LIEUTENANT
Yet I wish, sir,—
I mean for your particular,—you had not
Join'd in commission with him; but either
Had borne the action of yourself, or else
To him had left it solely.

AUFIDIUS
I understand thee well; and be thou sure,
when he shall come to his account, he knows not
What I can urge against him. Although it seems,
And so he thinks, and is no less apparent
To the vulgar eye, that he bears all things fairly.

And shows good husbandry for the Volscian state,
Fights dragon-like, and does achieve as soon
As draw his sword; yet he hath left undone
That which shall break his neck or hazard mine,
Whene'er we come to our account.

LIEUTENANT
Sir, I beseech you, think you he'll carry Rome?

AUFIDIUS
All places yield to him ere he sits down;
And the nobility of Rome are his:
The senators and patricians love him too:
The tribunes are no soldiers; and their people
Will be as rash in the repeal, as hasty
To expel him thence. I think he'll be to Rome
As is the osprey to the fish, who takes it
By sovereignty of nature. First he was
A noble servant to them; but he could not
Carry his honours even: whether 'twas pride,
Which out of daily fortune ever taints
The happy man; whether defect of judgment,
To fail in the disposing of those chances
Which he was lord of; or whether nature,
Not to be other than one thing, not moving
From the casque to the cushion, but commanding peace
Even with the same austerity and garb
As he controll'd the war; but one of these—
As he hath spices of them all, not all,
For I dare so far free him—made him fear'd,
So hated, and so banish'd: but he has a merit,
To choke it in the utterance. So our virtues
Lie in the interpretation of the time:
And power, unto itself most commendable,
Hath not a tomb so evident as a chair
To extol what it hath done.
One fire drives out one fire; one nail, one nail;
Rights by rights falter, strengths by strengths do fail.
Come, let's away. When, Caius, Rome is thine,
Thou art poor'st of all; then shortly art thou mine.

Exeunt

ACT V

SCENE I. Rome. A Public Place.

Enter MENENIUS, COMINIUS, SICINIUS, BRUTUS, and others

MENENIUS
No, I'll not go: you hear what he hath said
Which was sometime his general; who loved him
In a most dear particular. He call'd me father:
But what o' that? Go, you that banish'd him;
A mile before his tent fall down, and knee
The way into his mercy: nay, if he coy'd
To hear Cominius speak, I'll keep at home.

COMINIUS
He would not seem to know me.

MENENIUS
Do you hear?

COMINIUS
Yet one time he did call me by my name:
I urged our old acquaintance, and the drops
That we have bled together. Coriolanus
He would not answer to: forbad all names;
He was a kind of nothing, titleless,
Till he had forged himself a name o' the fire
Of burning Rome.

MENENIUS
Why, so: you have made good work!
A pair of tribunes that have rack'd for Rome,
To make coals cheap,—a noble memory!

COMINIUS
I minded him how royal 'twas to pardon
When it was less expected: he replied,
It was a bare petition of a state
To one whom they had punish'd.

MENENIUS
Very well:
Could he say less?

COMINIUS
I offer'd to awaken his regard
For's private friends: his answer to me was,
He could not stay to pick them in a pile
Of noisome musty chaff: he said 'twas folly,
For one poor grain or two, to leave unburnt,
And still to nose the offence.

MENENIUS
For one poor grain or two!
I am one of those; his mother, wife, his child,
And this brave fellow too, we are the grains:

You are the musty chaff; and you are smelt
Above the moon: we must be burnt for you.

SICINIUS
Nay, pray, be patient: if you refuse your aid
In this so never-needed help, yet do not
Upbraid's with our distress. But, sure, if you
Would be your country's pleader, your good tongue,
More than the instant army we can make,
Might stop our countryman.

MENENIUS
No, I'll not meddle.

SICINIUS
Pray you, go to him.

MENENIUS
What should I do?

BRUTUS
Only make trial what your love can do
For Rome, towards Marcius.

MENENIUS
Well, and say that Marcius
Return me, as Cominius is return'd,
Unheard; what then?
But as a discontented friend, grief-shot
With his unkindness? say't be so?

SICINIUS
Yet your good will
must have that thanks from Rome, after the measure
As you intended well.

MENENIUS
I'll undertake 't:
I think he'll hear me. Yet, to bite his lip
And hum at good Cominius, much unhearts me.
He was not taken well; he had not dined:
The veins unfill'd, our blood is cold, and then
We pout upon the morning, are unapt
To give or to forgive; but when we have stuff'd
These and these conveyances of our blood
With wine and feeding, we have suppler souls
Than in our priest-like fasts: therefore I'll watch him
Till he be dieted to my request,
And then I'll set upon him.

BRUTUS

You know the very road into his kindness,
And cannot lose your way.

MENENIUS
Good faith, I'll prove him,
Speed how it will. I shall ere long have knowledge
Of my success.

Exit

COMINIUS
He'll never hear him.

SICINIUS
Not?

COMINIUS
I tell you, he does sit in gold, his eye
Red as 'twould burn Rome; and his injury
The gaoler to his pity. I kneel'd before him;
'Twas very faintly he said 'Rise;' dismiss'd me
Thus, with his speechless hand: what he would do,
He sent in writing after me; what he would not,
Bound with an oath to yield to his conditions:
So that all hope is vain.
Unless his noble mother, and his wife;
Who, as I hear, mean to solicit him
For mercy to his country. Therefore, let's hence,
And with our fair entreaties haste them on.

Exeunt

SCENE II. Entrance of the Volscian Camp Before Rome.

Two Sentinels on guard.

Enter to them, MENENIUS

FIRST SENATOR
Stay: whence are you?

SECOND SENATOR
Stand, and go back.

MENENIUS
You guard like men; 'tis well: but, by your leave,
I am an officer of state, and come
To speak with Coriolanus.

FIRST SENATOR

From whence?

MENENIUS
From Rome.

FIRST SENATOR
You may not pass, you must return: our general
Will no more hear from thence.

SECOND SENATOR
You'll see your Rome embraced with fire before
You'll speak with Coriolanus.

MENENIUS
Good my friends,
If you have heard your general talk of Rome,
And of his friends there, it is lots to blanks,
My name hath touch'd your ears it is Menenius.

FIRST SENATOR
Be it so; go back: the virtue of your name
Is not here passable.

MENENIUS
I tell thee, fellow,
The general is my lover: I have been
The book of his good acts, whence men have read
His name unparallel'd, haply amplified;
For I have ever verified my friends,
Of whom he's chief, with all the size that verity
Would without lapsing suffer: nay, sometimes,
Like to a bowl upon a subtle ground,
I have tumbled past the throw; and in his praise
Have almost stamp'd the leasing: therefore, fellow,
I must have leave to pass.

FIRST SENATOR
Faith, sir, if you had told as many lies in his behalf as you have uttered words in your own, you
should not pass here; no, though it were as virtuous to lie as to live chastely. Therefore, go back.

MENENIUS
Prithee, fellow, remember my name is Menenius, always factionary on the party of your general.

SECOND SENATOR
Howsoever you have been his liar, as you say you have, I am one that, telling true under him, must
say, you cannot pass. Therefore, go back.

MENENIUS
Has he dined, canst thou tell? for I would not
speak with him till after dinner.

FIRST SENATOR
You are a Roman, are you?

MENENIUS
I am, as thy general is.

FIRST SENATOR
Then you should hate Rome, as he does. Can you, when you have pushed out your gates the very defender of them, and, in a violent popular ignorance, given your enemy your shield, think to front his revenges with the easy groans of old women, the virginal palms of your daughters, or with the palsied intercession of such a decayed dotant as you seem to be? Can you think to blow out the intended fire your city is ready to flame in, with such weak breath as this? No, you are deceived; therefore, back to Rome, and prepare for your execution: you are condemned, our general has sworn you out of reprieve and pardon.

MENENIUS
Sirrah, if thy captain knew I were here, he would use me with estimation.

SECOND SENATOR
Come, my captain knows you not.

MENENIUS
I mean, thy general.

FIRST SENATOR
My general cares not for you. Back, I say, go; lest I let forth your half-pint of blood; back,—that's the utmost of your having: back.

MENENIUS
Nay, but, fellow, fellow,—

Enter CORIOLANUS and AUFIDIUS

CORIOLANUS
What's the matter?

MENENIUS
Now, you companion, I'll say an errand for you: You shall know now that I am in estimation; you shall perceive that a Jack guardant cannot office me from my son Coriolanus: guess, but by my entertainment with him, if thou standest not i' the state of hanging, or of some death more long in spectatorship, and crueller in suffering; behold now presently, and swoon for what's to come upon thee.

To CORIOLANUS

The glorious gods sit in hourly synod about thy particular prosperity, and love thee no worse than thy old father Menenius does! O my son, my son! thou art preparing fire for us; look thee, here's water to quench it. I was hardly moved to come to thee; but being assured none but myself could move thee, I have been blown out of your gates with sighs; and conjure thee to pardon Rome, and thy petitionary countrymen. The good gods assuage thy wrath, and turn the dregs of it upon this varlet here,—this, who, like a block, hath denied my access to thee.

CORIOLANUS
Away!

MENENIUS
How! away!

CORIOLANUS
Wife, mother, child, I know not. My affairs
Are servanted to others: though I owe
My revenge properly, my remission lies
In Volscian breasts. That we have been familiar,
Ingrate forgetfulness shall poison, rather
Than pity note how much. Therefore, be gone.
Mine ears against your suits are stronger than
Your gates against my force. Yet, for I loved thee,
Take this along; I writ it for thy sake

Gives a letter

And would have rent it. Another word, Menenius,
I will not hear thee speak. This man, Aufidius,
Was my beloved in Rome: yet thou behold'st!

AUFIDIUS
You keep a constant temper.

Exeunt CORIOLANUS and AUFIDIUS

FIRST SENATOR
Now, sir, is your name Menenius?

SECOND SENATOR
'Tis a spell, you see, of much power: you know the way home again.

FIRST SENATOR
Do you hear how we are shent for keeping your greatness back?

SECOND SENATOR
What cause, do you think, I have to swoon?

MENENIUS
I neither care for the world nor your general: for such things as you, I can scarce think there's any, ye're so slight. He that hath a will to die by himself fears it not from another: let your general do his worst. For you, be that you are, long; and your misery increase with your age! I say to you, as I was said to, Away!

Exit

FIRST SENATOR
A noble fellow, I warrant him.

SECOND SENATOR
The worthy fellow is our general: he's the rock, the oak not to be wind-shaken.

Exeunt

SCENE III. The Tent of Coriolanus.

Enter CORIOLANUS, AUFIDIUS, and others

CORIOLANUS
We will before the walls of Rome tomorrow
Set down our host. My partner in this action,
You must report to the Volscian lords, how plainly
I have borne this business.

AUFIDIUS
Only their ends
You have respected; stopp'd your ears against
The general suit of Rome; never admitted
A private whisper, no, not with such friends
That thought them sure of you.

CORIOLANUS
This last old man,
Whom with a crack'd heart I have sent to Rome,
Loved me above the measure of a father;
Nay, godded me, indeed. Their latest refuge
Was to send him; for whose old love I have,
Though I show'd sourly to him, once more offer'd
The first conditions, which they did refuse
And cannot now accept; to grace him only
That thought he could do more, a very little
I have yielded to: fresh embassies and suits,
Nor from the state nor private friends, hereafter
Will I lend ear to. Ha! what shout is this?

Shout within
Shall I be tempted to infringe my vow
In the same time 'tis made? I will not.

Enter in mourning habits, VIRGILIA, VOLUMNIA, leading young MARCIUS, VALERIA, and Attendants

My wife comes foremost; then the honour'd mould
Wherein this trunk was framed, and in her hand
The grandchild to her blood. But, out, affection!
All bond and privilege of nature, break!
Let it be virtuous to be obstinate.
What is that curt'sy worth? or those doves' eyes,
Which can make gods forsworn? I melt, and am not

Of stronger earth than others. My mother bows;
As if Olympus to a molehill should
In supplication nod: and my young boy
Hath an aspect of intercession, which
Great nature cries 'Deny not.' let the Volsces
Plough Rome and harrow Italy: I'll never
Be such a gosling to obey instinct, but stand,
As if a man were author of himself
And knew no other kin.

VIRGILIA
My lord and husband!

CORIOLANUS
These eyes are not the same I wore in Rome.

VIRGILIA
The sorrow that delivers us thus changed
Makes you think so.

CORIOLANUS
Like a dull actor now,
I have forgot my part, and I am out,
Even to a full disgrace. Best of my flesh,
Forgive my tyranny; but do not say
For that 'Forgive our Romans.' O, a kiss
Long as my exile, sweet as my revenge!
Now, by the jealous queen of heaven, that kiss
I carried from thee, dear; and my true lip
Hath virgin'd it e'er since. You gods! I prate,
And the most noble mother of the world
Leave unsaluted: sink, my knee, i' the earth;

Kneels

Of thy deep duty more impression show
Than that of common sons.

VOLUMNIA
O, stand up blest!
Whilst, with no softer cushion than the flint,
I kneel before thee; and unproperly
Show duty, as mistaken all this while
Between the child and parent.

Kneels

CORIOLANUS
What is this?
Your knees to me? to your corrected son?
Then let the pebbles on the hungry beach

Fillip the stars; then let the mutinous winds
Strike the proud cedars 'gainst the fiery sun;
Murdering impossibility, to make
What cannot be, slight work.

VOLUMNIA
Thou art my warrior;
I holp to frame thee. Do you know this lady?

CORIOLANUS
The noble sister of Publicola,
The moon of Rome, chaste as the icicle
That's curdied by the frost from purest snow
And hangs on Dian's temple: dear Valeria!

VOLUMNIA
This is a poor epitome of yours,
Which by the interpretation of full time
May show like all yourself.

CORIOLANUS
The god of soldiers,
With the consent of supreme Jove, inform
Thy thoughts with nobleness; that thou mayst prove
To shame unvulnerable, and stick i' the wars
Like a great sea-mark, standing every flaw,
And saving those that eye thee!

VOLUMNIA
Your knee, sirrah.

CORIOLANUS
That's my brave boy!

VOLUMNIA
Even he, your wife, this lady, and myself,
Are suitors to you.

CORIOLANUS
I beseech you, peace:
Or, if you'ld ask, remember this before:
The thing I have forsworn to grant may never
Be held by you denials. Do not bid me
Dismiss my soldiers, or capitulate
Again with Rome's mechanics: tell me not
Wherein I seem unnatural: desire not
To ally my rages and revenges with
Your colder reasons.

VOLUMNIA

O, no more, no more!
You have said you will not grant us any thing;
For we have nothing else to ask, but that
Which you deny already: yet we will ask;
That, if you fail in our request, the blame
May hang upon your hardness: therefore hear us.

CORIOLANUS
Aufidius, and you Volsces, mark; for we'll
Hear nought from Rome in private. Your request?

VOLUMNIA
Should we be silent and not speak, our raiment
And state of bodies would bewray what life
We have led since thy exile. Think with thyself
How more unfortunate than all living women
Are we come hither: since that thy sight, which should
Make our eyes flow with joy, hearts dance with comforts,
Constrains them weep and shake with fear and sorrow;
Making the mother, wife and child to see
The son, the husband and the father tearing
His country's bowels out. And to poor we
Thine enmity's most capital: thou barr'st us
Our prayers to the gods, which is a comfort
That all but we enjoy; for how can we,
Alas, how can we for our country pray.
Whereto we are bound, together with thy victory,
Whereto we are bound? alack, or we must lose
The country, our dear nurse, or else thy person,
Our comfort in the country. We must find
An evident calamity, though we had
Our wish, which side should win: for either thou
Must, as a foreign recreant, be led
With manacles thorough our streets, or else
triumphantly tread on thy country's ruin,
And bear the palm for having bravely shed
Thy wife and children's blood. For myself, son,
I purpose not to wait on fortune till
These wars determine: if I cannot persuade thee
Rather to show a noble grace to both parts
Than seek the end of one, thou shalt no sooner
March to assault thy country than to tread—
Trust to't, thou shalt not—on thy mother's womb,
That brought thee to this world.

VIRGILIA
Ay, and mine,
That brought you forth this boy, to keep your name
Living to time.

Young MARCIUS

A' shall not tread on me;
I'll run away till I am bigger, but then I'll fight.

CORIOLANUS
Not of a woman's tenderness to be,
Requires nor child nor woman's face to see.
I have sat too long.

Rising

VOLUMNIA
Nay, go not from us thus.
If it were so that our request did tend
To save the Romans, thereby to destroy
The Volsces whom you serve, you might condemn us,
As poisonous of your honour: no; our suit
Is that you reconcile them: while the Volsces
May say 'This mercy we have show'd;' the Romans,
'This we received;' and each in either side
Give the all-hail to thee and cry 'Be blest
For making up this peace!' Thou know'st, great son,
The end of war's uncertain, but this certain,
That, if thou conquer Rome, the benefit
Which thou shalt thereby reap is such a name,
Whose repetition will be dogg'd with curses;
Whose chronicle thus writ: 'The man was noble,
But with his last attempt he wiped it out;
Destroy'd his country, and his name remains
To the ensuing age abhorr'd.' Speak to me, son:
Thou hast affected the fine strains of honour,
To imitate the graces of the gods;
To tear with thunder the wide cheeks o' the air,
And yet to charge thy sulphur with a bolt
That should but rive an oak. Why dost not speak?
Think'st thou it honourable for a noble man
Still to remember wrongs? Daughter, speak you:
He cares not for your weeping. Speak thou, boy:
Perhaps thy childishness will move him more
Than can our reasons. There's no man in the world
More bound to 's mother; yet here he lets me prate
Like one i' the stocks. Thou hast never in thy life
Show'd thy dear mother any courtesy,
When she, poor hen, fond of no second brood,
Has cluck'd thee to the wars and safely home,
Loaden with honour. Say my request's unjust,
And spurn me back: but if it be not so,
Thou art not honest; and the gods will plague thee,
That thou restrain'st from me the duty which
To a mother's part belongs. He turns away:
Down, ladies; let us shame him with our knees.
To his surname Coriolanus 'longs more pride

Than pity to our prayers. Down: an end;
This is the last: so we will home to Rome,
And die among our neighbours. Nay, behold 's:
This boy, that cannot tell what he would have
But kneels and holds up bands for fellowship,
Does reason our petition with more strength
Than thou hast to deny 't. Come, let us go:
This fellow had a Volscian to his mother;
His wife is in Corioli and his child
Like him by chance. Yet give us our dispatch:
I am hush'd until our city be a-fire,
And then I'll speak a little.

He holds her by the hand, silent

CORIOLANUS
O mother, mother!
What have you done? Behold, the heavens do ope,
The gods look down, and this unnatural scene
They laugh at. O my mother, mother! O!
You have won a happy victory to Rome;
But, for your son,—believe it, O, believe it,
Most dangerously you have with him prevail'd,
If not most mortal to him. But, let it come.
Aufidius, though I cannot make true wars,
I'll frame convenient peace. Now, good Aufidius,
Were you in my stead, would you have heard
A mother less? or granted less, Aufidius?

AUFIDIUS
I was moved withal.

CORIOLANUS
I dare be sworn you were:
And, sir, it is no little thing to make
Mine eyes to sweat compassion. But, good sir,
What peace you'll make, advise me: for my part,
I'll not to Rome, I'll back with you; and pray you,
Stand to me in this cause. O mother! wife!

AUFIDIUS
[Aside] I am glad thou hast set thy mercy and thy honour
At difference in thee: out of that I'll work
Myself a former fortune.

The LADIES make signs to CORIOLANUS

CORIOLANUS
Ay, by and by;

To VOLUMNIA, VIRGILIA, & c

But we will drink together; and you shall bear
A better witness back than words, which we,
On like conditions, will have counter-seal'd.
Come, enter with us. Ladies, you deserve
To have a temple built you: all the swords
In Italy, and her confederate arms,
Could not have made this peace.

Exeunt

SCENE IV. Rome. A Public Place.

Enter MENENIUS and SICINIUS

MENENIUS
See you yond coign o' the Capitol, yond
corner-stone?

SICINIUS
Why, what of that?

MENENIUS
If it be possible for you to displace it with your little finger, there is some hope the ladies of Rome, especially his mother, may prevail with him. But I say there is no hope in't: our throats are sentenced and stay upon execution.

SICINIUS
Is't possible that so short a time can alter the condition of a man!

MENENIUS
There is differency between a grub and a butterfly; yet your butterfly was a grub. This Marcius is grown from man to dragon: he has wings; he's more than a creeping thing.

SICINIUS
He loved his mother dearly.

MENENIUS
So did he me: and he no more remembers his mother now than an eight-year-old horse. The tartness of his face sours ripe grapes: when he walks, he moves like an engine, and the ground shrinks before his treading: he is able to pierce a corslet with his eye; talks like a knell, and his hum is a battery. He sits in his state, as a thing made for Alexander. What he bids be done is finished with his bidding. He wants nothing of a god but eternity and a heaven to throne in.

SICINIUS
Yes, mercy, if you report him truly.

MENENIUS
I paint him in the character. Mark what mercy his mother shall bring from him: there is no more mercy in him than there is milk in a male tiger; that shall our poor city find: and all this is long of you.

SICINIUS
The gods be good unto us!

MENENIUS
No, in such a case the gods will not be good unto us. When we banished him, we respected not them; and, he returning to break our necks, they respect not us.

Enter a MESSENGER

MESSENGER
Sir, if you'ld save your life, fly to your house:
The plebeians have got your fellow-tribune
And hale him up and down, all swearing, if
The Roman ladies bring not comfort home,
They'll give him death by inches.

Enter a SECOND MESSENGER

SICINIUS
What's the news?

SECOND MESSENGER
Good news, good news; the ladies have prevail'd,
The Volscians are dislodged, and Marcius gone:
A merrier day did never yet greet Rome,
No, not the expulsion of the Tarquins.

SICINIUS
Friend,
Art thou certain this is true? is it most certain?

SECOND MESSENGER
As certain as I know the sun is fire:
Where have you lurk'd, that you make doubt of it?
Ne'er through an arch so hurried the blown tide,
As the recomforted through the gates. Why, hark you!

Trumpets; hautboys; drums beat; all together

The trumpets, sackbuts, psalteries and fifes,
Tabours and cymbals and the shouting Romans,
Make the sun dance. Hark you!

A shout within

MENENIUS
This is good news:
I will go meet the ladies. This Volumnia
Is worth of consuls, senators, patricians,
A city full; of tribunes, such as you,

A sea and land full. You have pray'd well to-day:
This morning for ten thousand of your throats
I'd not have given a doit. Hark, how they joy!

Music still, with shouts

SICINIUS
First, the gods bless you for your tidings; next,
Accept my thankfulness.

SECOND MESSENGER
Sir, we have all
Great cause to give great thanks.

SICINIUS
They are near the city?

SECOND MESSENGER
Almost at point to enter.

SICINIUS
We will meet them,
And help the joy.

Exeunt

SCENE V. The Same. A Street Near the Gate.

Enter two SENATORS with VOLUMNIA, VIRGILIA, VALERIA, & c. passing over the stage, followed by PATRICIANS and others

FIRST SENATOR
Behold our patroness, the life of Rome!
Call all your tribes together, praise the gods,
And make triumphant fires; strew flowers before them:
Unshout the noise that banish'd Marcius,
Repeal him with the welcome of his mother;
Cry 'Welcome, ladies, welcome!'

ALL
Welcome, ladies, Welcome!

A flourish with drums and trumpets.

Exeunt

SCENE VI. Antium. A Public Place.

Enter TULLUS AUFIDIUS, with ATTENDANTS

AUFIDIUS
Go tell the lords o' the city I am here:
Deliver them this paper: having read it,
Bid them repair to the market place; where I,
Even in theirs and in the commons' ears,
Will vouch the truth of it. Him I accuse
The city ports by this hath enter'd and
Intends to appear before the people, hoping
To purge herself with words: dispatch.

Exeunt ATTENDANTS

Enter three or four CONSPIRATORS of AUFIDIUS' faction

Most welcome!

FIRST CONSPIRATOR
How is it with our general?

AUFIDIUS
Even so
As with a man by his own alms empoison'd,
And with his charity slain.

SECOND CONSPIRATOR
Most noble sir,
If you do hold the same intent wherein
You wish'd us parties, we'll deliver you
Of your great danger.

AUFIDIUS
Sir, I cannot tell:
We must proceed as we do find the people.

THIRD CONSPIRATOR
The people will remain uncertain whilst
'Twixt you there's difference; but the fall of either
Makes the survivor heir of all.

AUFIDIUS
I know it;
And my pretext to strike at him admits
A good construction. I raised him, and I pawn'd
Mine honour for his truth: who being so heighten'd,
He water'd his new plants with dews of flattery,
Seducing so my friends; and, to this end,
He bow'd his nature, never known before
But to be rough, unswayable and free.

THIRD CONSPIRATOR
Sir, his stoutness
When he did stand for consul, which he lost
By lack of stooping,—

AUFIDIUS
That I would have spoke of:
Being banish'd for't, he came unto my hearth;
Presented to my knife his throat: I took him;
Made him joint-servant with me; gave him way
In all his own desires; nay, let him choose
Out of my files, his projects to accomplish,
My best and freshest men; served his designments
In mine own person; holp to reap the fame
Which he did end all his; and took some pride
To do myself this wrong: till, at the last,
I seem'd his follower, not partner, and
He waged me with his countenance, as if
I had been mercenary.

FIRST CONSPIRATOR
So he did, my lord:
The army marvell'd at it, and, in the last,
When he had carried Rome and that we look'd
For no less spoil than glory,—

AUFIDIUS
There was it:
For which my sinews shall be stretch'd upon him.
At a few drops of women's rheum, which are
As cheap as lies, he sold the blood and labour
Of our great action: therefore shall he die,
And I'll renew me in his fall. But, hark!

Drums and trumpets sound, with great shouts of the People

FIRST CONSPIRATOR
Your native town you enter'd like a post,
And had no welcomes home: but he returns,
Splitting the air with noise.

SECOND CONSPIRATOR
And patient fools,
Whose children he hath slain, their base throats tear
With giving him glory.

THIRD CONSPIRATOR
Therefore, at your vantage,
Ere he express himself, or move the people
With what he would say, let him feel your sword,
Which we will second. When he lies along,

After your way his tale pronounced shall bury
His reasons with his body.

AUFIDIUS
Say no more:
Here come the lords.

Enter the LORDS of the city

ALL THE LORDS
You are most welcome home.

AUFIDIUS
I have not deserved it.
But, worthy lords, have you with heed perused
What I have written to you?

LORDS
We have.

FIRST LORD
And grieve to hear't.
What faults he made before the last, I think
Might have found easy fines: but there to end
Where he was to begin and give away
The benefit of our levies, answering us
With our own charge, making a treaty where
There was a yielding,—this admits no excuse.

AUFIDIUS
He approaches: you shall hear him.

Enter CORIOLANUS, marching with drum and colours; commoners being with him

CORIOLANUS
Hail, lords! I am return'd your soldier,
No more infected with my country's love
Than when I parted hence, but still subsisting
Under your great command. You are to know
That prosperously I have attempted and
With bloody passage led your wars even to
The gates of Rome. Our spoils we have brought home
Do more than counterpoise a full third part
The charges of the action. We have made peace
With no less honour to the Antiates
Than shame to the Romans: and we here deliver,
Subscribed by the consuls and patricians,
Together with the seal o' the senate, what
We have compounded on.

AUFIDIUS

Read it not, noble lords;
But tell the traitor, in the high'st degree
He hath abused your powers.

CORIOLANUS
Traitor! how now!

AUFIDIUS
Ay, traitor, Marcius!

CORIOLANUS
Marcius!

AUFIDIUS
Ay, Marcius, Caius Marcius: dost thou think
I'll grace thee with that robbery, thy stol'n name
Coriolanus in Corioli?
You lords and heads o' the state, perfidiously
He has betray'd your business, and given up,
For certain drops of salt, your city Rome,
I say 'your city,' to his wife and mother;
Breaking his oath and resolution like
A twist of rotten silk, never admitting
Counsel o' the war, but at his nurse's tears
He whined and roar'd away your victory,
That pages blush'd at him and men of heart
Look'd wondering each at other.

CORIOLANUS
Hear'st thou, Mars?

AUFIDIUS
Name not the god, thou boy of tears!

CORIOLANUS
Ha!

AUFIDIUS
No more.

CORIOLANUS
Measureless liar, thou hast made my heart
Too great for what contains it. Boy! O slave!
Pardon me, lords, 'tis the first time that ever
I was forced to scold. Your judgments, my grave lords,
Must give this cur the lie: and his own notion—
Who wears my stripes impress'd upon him; that
Must bear my beating to his grave—shall join
To thrust the lie unto him.

FIRST LORD

Peace, both, and hear me speak.

CORIOLANUS
Cut me to pieces, Volsces; men and lads,
Stain all your edges on me. Boy! false hound!
If you have writ your annals true, 'tis there,
That, like an eagle in a dove-cote, I
Flutter'd your Volscians in Corioli:
Alone I did it. Boy!

AUFIDIUS
Why, noble lords,
Will you be put in mind of his blind fortune,
Which was your shame, by this unholy braggart,
'Fore your own eyes and ears?

ALL CONSPIRATORS
Let him die for't.

ALL THE PEOPLE
'Tear him to pieces.' 'Do it presently.' 'He kill'd
my son.' 'My daughter.' 'He killed my cousin
Marcus.' 'He killed my father.'

SECOND LORD
Peace, ho! no outrage: peace!
The man is noble and his fame folds-in
This orb o' the earth. His last offences to us
Shall have judicious hearing. Stand, Aufidius,
And trouble not the peace.

CORIOLANUS
O that I had him,
With six Aufidiuses, or more, his tribe,
To use my lawful sword!

AUFIDIUS
Insolent villain!

ALL CONSPIRATORS
Kill, kill, kill, kill, kill him!

The CONSPIRATORS draw, and kill CORIOLANUS: AUFIDIUS stands on his body

LORDS
Hold, hold, hold, hold!

AUFIDIUS
My noble masters, hear me speak.

FIRST LORD

O Tullus,—

SECOND LORD
Thou hast done a deed whereat valour will weep.

THIRD LORD
Tread not upon him. Masters all, be quiet;
Put up your swords.

AUFIDIUS
My lords, when you shall know—as in this rage,
Provoked by him, you cannot—the great danger
Which this man's life did owe you, you'll rejoice
That he is thus cut off. Please it your honours
To call me to your senate, I'll deliver
Myself your loyal servant, or endure
Your heaviest censure.

FIRST LORD
Bear from hence his body;
And mourn you for him: let him be regarded
As the most noble corse that ever herald
Did follow to his urn.

SECOND LORD
His own impatience
Takes from Aufidius a great part of blame.
Let's make the best of it.

AUFIDIUS
My rage is gone;
And I am struck with sorrow. Take him up.
Help, three o' the chiefest soldiers; I'll be one.
Beat thou the drum, that it speak mournfully:
Trail your steel pikes. Though in this city he
Hath widow'd and unchilded many a one,
Which to this hour bewail the injury,
Yet he shall have a noble memory. Assist.

Exeunt, bearing the body of CORIOLANUS. A dead march sounded

William Shakespeare – A Short Biography

The life of William Shakespeare, arguably the most significant figure in the Western literary canon, is relatively unknown. Even the exact date of his birth is uncertain. April 23rd, the date now generally accepted to be the date of his birth, is a result of a scholarly mistake and the appealing coincidence of its being also the day of his death.

That so little is known about a writer with such great literary scope and accomplishment has naturally invited speculation and conspiracy theories about the authenticity of his authorship, his influence and even his existence.

Shakespeare was born in Stratford-upon-Avon in 1565, possibly on the 23rd April, St. George's Day, and baptised there on 26th April. His father was John Shakespeare, a successful glover and alderman who hailed from Snitterfield. His mother was Mary Arden, whose father was an affluent landowner. In total their union bore eight children; William was the third of these and the eldest surviving son.

Although there is no hard evidence on his education it is widely agreed among scholars that William attended the King's New School in Stratford which was chartered as a free school in 1553. This school was only a quarter of a mile from the house in which he spent his childhood, but since there are no attendance records existing it is assumed, rather than known, this was the base for his education.

Although the quality of education in a grammar school at that time varied wildly the curriculum did not, a key aspect of which, by royal decree, was Latin, and it is undoubtable that the school will have delivered an intensive education in Latin grammar, drawing heavily on the work of the classical Latin authors. If Shakespeare did attend this school then it is very likely the starting point for the fascination with and extensive knowledge of the classical Latin authors which would inform and inspire so much of his work began.

Little more detail is known of William's childhood, or his early teenage years, until, at the age of 18, he married Anne Hathaway, who was 26 and from the nearby village of Shottery. Her father was a yeoman farmer, and their family home a small farmhouse in the village. In his will he left her £6 13s 4d, six pounds, thirteen shillings and fourpence, to be paid on her wedding day. On November 27th, 1582 the consistory court of the Diocese of Worcester issued a marriage licence, and on the 28th two of Hathaway's neighbours, Fulk Sandells and John Richardson, posted bonds which guaranteed that there were no lawful claims to impede the marriage along with a surety of £40 to act as a financial guarantee for the wedding.

The marriage was conducted in some haste since, unusually, the marriage banns were read only once instead of the more normal three times, a decision which would have been taken by the Worcester chancellor. This haste is no doubt due to the child Anne delivered their first child, Susanna, six months later. Susanna, was baptised on May 26th, 1583. Several scholars have voiced their opinion that the wedding was imposed on a reluctant Shakespeare by Hathaway's outraged parents, although, again, there is nothing to formally support the theory. It has been further argued that the circumstances surrounding the wedding, particularly those of the neighbourly assurances, indicate that Shakespeare was involved with two women at the time of his marriage. According to the theory proposed by the early twentieth century scholar Frank Harris, Shakespeare had already chosen to marry a woman named Anne Whateley. It was only once this proposed union became known that Hathaway's outraged family forced him to marry their daughter. Harris goes on to surmise that Shakespeare considered the affair entrapment, and that this led to his wholesale despising of her, a "loathing for his wife [which] was measureless" and which ultimately caused him to leave Stratford and her and make for the theatre. But equally other scholars such as John Aubrey have responded to this with evidence that Shakespeare returned to Stratford every year which, if true, would rather diminish Harris's claim that Hathaway had poisoned Stratford for Shakespeare.

Harris's theory aside, Shakespeare and Hathaway had two more children, twins Hamnet and Judith, baptised on February 2nd,1585. Hamnet, Shakespeare's only son, died during one of the frequent outbreaks of bubonic plague and was buried on the August 11th, 1596, at the age of only eleven.

Little is known of Shakespeare's life during the years following the birth of the twins until he appears mentioned in relation to the London theatres in 1592, apart from a fleeting mention in the complaints bill of a legal case which came before the Queen's Bench court at Westminster, dated Michaelmas Term 1588 and October 9th, 1589. Despite this period of time being referred to in scholarly circles as Shakespeare's "lost years", there are several stories, apocryphal in nature, which are attributed to Shakespeare. For example, there is a legend in Stratford that he fled the town in order to avoid prosecution for poaching deer on the estate of Thomas Lucy, a local squire. It is also supposed that Shakespeare went so far as to take revenge on Lucy, a politician whose Protestantism opposed Shakespeare's Catholic childhood, by writing the following lampooning ballad about him:

> A parliament member, a justice of peace,
> At home a poor scarecrow, at London an ass,
> If lousy is Lucy as some folks miscall it
> Then Lucy is lousy whatever befall it.

However amusing the ballad and legend may be in imagining the life of a young Shakespeare, youthfully mischievous and still developing the wit, sense of adventure and humour which would become integral aspects of his writing, there is simply no evidence either to support the theory or to suggest that Shakespeare penned the ballad. Alongside this are suggestions that he began his theatrical career while minding the horses of the patrons of the London theatres and that he spent some time as a schoolmaster employed by one Alexander Hoghton, a Catholic landowner in Lancashire, in whose will is named "William Shakeshafte". However, this was a popular name in the Lancashire area at that time and there is no evidence that this referred to Shakespeare. The wealth of his writing makes it a frustrating exercise to learn more of his life and the manner in which he achieved those outstanding and lionized works.

Interestingly, the reference to Shakespeare in 1592 which ends the "lost years" is a piece of theatrical criticism by playwright Robert Greene in *Groats-Worth of Wit*. In a scathing passage Greene writes "…there is an upstart Crow, beautified with our feathers, that with his *Tiger's heart wrapped in a Player's hide*, supposes he is as well able to bombast out a blank verse as the best of you: and being an absolute *Johannes factotum*, is in his own conceit the only Shake-scene in a country." From this entry we can make some important inferences which shed light on Shakespeare's career, the first of which is that to be acknowledged, even negatively, by a playwright such as Robert Greene, by this point he must have been making significant impact on the London stage as a writer. Also of significance is the very meaning of the words themselves, for it is generally acknowledged that Shakespeare is being accused of writing with a lofty ambition beyond his capabilities and, more importantly, the capabilities of his contemporaries who were educated at Oxford and Cambridge. Within this remark, then, is an inherent snobbery which Shakespeare would come to resent and ultimately challenge in his writing. Though Greene's parody of "Oh, tiger's heart wrapped in a woman's hide" makes reference to *Henry VI, Part 3*, it is likely that Greene's opinion of Shakespeare was in part informed by another of Shakespeare's plays which was heavily criticised, *Titus Adronicus*, believed to have been written between 1588 and 1593. It was his first attempt at tragedy, almost prototypical, and was written at a time when, according to the scholar Jonathan Bate, he was "experimenting with ways of writing about and representing rape and seduction". Drawing heavily on the sixth book of Ovid's *Metamorphoses* as its main source of inspiration for the rape and mutilation of Lavinia, it offended the sensibilities of the more highbrow members of its audience, whilst presumably also simultaneously intimidating them with its detailed knowledge of

Ovid, a writer typically considered the reserve of the university-educated. Not only, then, was Shakespeare demonstrating a knowledge of classical literature which they thought befitted only a traditional scholar and thereby shining a light to the snobbery and exclusivity of such an education, but he was doing it radically and brilliantly.

By 1594 the Lord Chamberlain's Men had recognised his worthiness as a playwright and were performing his works. With the advantage of Shakespeare's progressive writing they rapidly became London's leading company of players, affording him more exposure and, following the death of Queen Elizabeth in 1603, a royal patent by the new king, James I, at which point they changed their name to the King's Men.

Before this success, though, several company members had formed a partnership to build their own theatre which came to be on the south bank of the river Thames, the now-famous and reconstructed Globe theatre. Though it is unclear precisely what Shakespeare's involvement in this venture was, records of his property and investments indicate that he came to be rich during this period, buying the second-largest house in Stratford, called New Place, in 1597, which he made his family home. Prior to this he was living in the parish of St Helen's Bishopsgate, north of the River Thames. He continued to spend most of his time at work in London and from about 1598-1602, he seems to have lived in the Paris Gardens area of Bankside south of the river near The Globe.

Despite efforts to pirate his work, Shakespeare's name was by 1598 so well known that it had already become a selling point in its own right on title pages.

An interesting aside is that theatres were mostly constructed on the south bank of the Thames (then part of the county of Surrey) as performing in London itself was thought to be a bad influence on the masses and subject to periodic bouts of censorship, repression and closing of venues which in the City itself was mainly courtyards and open areas at the many Inns.

Excluded from the City purpose built theatres began to be constructed outside the City limits. This area of the Thames though was rough and naturally vibrant with all sorts of characters, many of them of dubious nature or even criminal. It was also prone, due to its over-crowding and bad sanitation, to bouts of bubonic plague and other diseases particularly during the summer which was a further reason for the theatres there being closed. The Curtain, The Rose, The Swan, The Fortune, The Blackfriars and of course The Globe were all purpose built and situated here, some with an audience capacity approaching 3,000.

The first known printed copies of Shakespeare's plays date from 1594 in quarto editions, though these quarto editions are often considered "bad", a term referring to the likelihood of specific quarto editions being based on, for example, a reconstruction of a play as it was witnessed, rather than Shakespeare's original manuscript. The best example of such memorial reconstruction can be found in the differences between the first and second quarto editions of *Hamlet*. In examining Hamlet's most famous soliloquy, "to be or not to be", we can immediately recognise significant differences. First, the familiar second quarto version:

> To be, or not to be; that is the question:
> Whether 'tis nobler in the mind to suffer
> The slings and arrows of outrageous fortune,
> Or to take arms against a sea of troubles,
> And, by opposing, end them.

And, by contrast, the first quarto version:

> To be, or not to be, I there's the point,
> To Die, to sleep, is that all? I all:

For scholar Henry David Gray the first quarto lines are emblematic of "a distorted version of the completed drama filled out and revised by an inferior poet" and based, he goes on to argue, on the fractured memories of the play as witnessed and performed by the actor playing Marcellus. Gray, and several other critics, consider the first quarto a pirated copy, printed in haste without the writer's permission in an attempt to make quick money following the success of the play in the theatre. In understanding the significance of Marcellus to the theory it is imperative to note that the authenticity of each quarto is based on its similarities to the version of the play found in the first folio, printed in 1623 and believed to be authorised by Shakespeare. Therefore, since in the folio version of *Hamlet* the "to be or not to be" soliloquy is virtually identical to that of the second quarto, it is believed that the second was authored by Shakespeare himself and that the first, by its considerable differences, must therefore be in some way compromised. However, when read in comparison to the folio version, the only character whose lines are almost entirely perfect are those spoken by Marcellus, which, since dramatic practice at the time was for actors to be given only their own lines and three or four word 'cues' based on the lines preceding theirs, suggests that the first quarto is a memorial reconstruction of the play written by the actor who played Marcellus. Having committed his own lines to memory he was able to reproduce them accurately, but was left to fill in the remaining lines and plot from memory which accounts for the truncated and often vastly inferior writing in the first quarto.

According to the remaining cast lists from the period, Shakespeare remained an actor throughout his career as a writer, and it is thought he continued to act after he retired his pen. In 1616 he is recorded in the cast list in Ben Jonson's collected *Works* in the plays *Man in His Humour* 1598) and *Sejanus His Fall* (1603), though some scholars consider his absence from the list of Jonson's *Volpone* evidence that, by 1605, his acting career was nearing its end. Despite this in the First Folio he is listed as one of "the Principle Actors in all these Plays", several of which were only staged after *Volpone*.

By 1604 he had moved again, remaining north of the river, to an area near St. Paul's Cathedral where he rented a fine room amongst fine houses from Christopher Mountjoy, a French hatmaker and Huguenot.

The Anglo-Welsh poet John Davies of Hereford wrote in 1610 that "good Will" tended to play "kingly" roles, suggesting he was still on stage, perhaps now performing the more mature kings such as Lear and Henry VI. There has even been the suggestion that Shakespeare played the ghost of Hamlet's father, though there is little evidence to suggest it.

In 1608 the King's Men purchased the Blackfriars theatre from Henry Evans, and according to Cuthbert Burbage, one of the most highly regarded actors of the time, "placed many players" there "which were Heminges, Condell, Shakespeare, etc." A 1609 lawsuit brought against John Addenbrooke in Stratford on the 7th of June describes Shakespeare as "generosus nuper in curia domini Jacobi" (a gentleman recently at the court of King James) which indicates that by this time he was spending more time in Stratford. A likely cause of this was the bubonic plague, frequent outbreaks of which demanded the equally frequent closing of places of public gathering, principle among which were the theatres. Between May 1603 and February 1610 the theatres were closed for a total of 60 months, meaning there was no acting work and nobody to perform new plays. Though in 1610 Shakespeare returned to Stratford and it is supposed lived with his wife, he made frequent visits to London between 1611-14, being called as a witness in the trial *Bellott v. Mountjoy*, a case addressing concerns about the marriage settlement of Mountjoy's daughter, Mary. In March 1613 he purchased a gatehouse in the former Blackfriars priory, and spent several weeks in the city with his son-in-law John Hall, a physician, married to his daughter Susanna, from November 1614.

No plays are attributed to Shakespeare after 1613, and the last few plays he wrote before this time were in collaboration with other writers, one of whom is likely to be John Fletcher who succeeded him as the house playwright for the King's Men.

In early 1616 his daughter Judith married Thomas Quiney, a vintner and tobacconist. He signed his last will and testament on March 25th, of the same year, and the following day Quiney was ordered to do public penance for having fathered an illegitimate child with a woman named Margaret Wheeler who had died during childbirth which had enabled Quiney to cover up the scandal. This public humiliation would have been embarrassing for Shakespeare and his family.

William Shakespeare died two months later on April 23rd, 1616, survived by his wife and two daughters.

According to his will the bulk of his considerable estate was left to his elder daughter Susanna, with the instruction that she pass it down intact to "the first son of her body". However, though Susanna and Judith had four children between them they all died without progeny, ending Shakespeare's direct lineage. Also in his will was the instruction that his "second best bed" be left to his wife Anne, likely an insult, though the bed was possibly matrimonial and therefore of significant sentimental value.

He was buried two days after his death in the chancel of the Holy Trinity Church in Stratford-Upon-Avon.

The epitaph on the slab which covers his grave includes the following passage,

> Good frend for Iesvs sake forbeare,
> To digg the dvst encloased heare.
> Bleste be ye man yt spares thes stones,
> And cvrst be he yt moves my bones

which, in modern translation, reads

> Good friend, for Jesus's sake forbear,
> To dig the dust enclosed here.
> Blessed be the man that spares these stones,
> And cursed be he that moves my bones.

At some point before 1623 there was a funerary monument erected in his memory on the north wall of Stratford-upon-Avon which features a half-effigy of him writing, and which likens him to Nestor, Socrates and Virgil.

On January 29th, 1741 a white marble memorial statue to him was erected in Poets' Corner in Westminster Abbey.

Though there have been many monuments built around the world in memory of Shakespeare, undoubtedly the greatest memorial of all is the body of work which became the foundation of Western literary canon and an inspiration for every generation.

William Shakespeare – A Concise Bibliography

1589	Comedy of Errors (Comedy)
1590	Henry VI, Part II (History) Henry VI, Part III (History)
1591	Henry VI, Part I (History)
1592	Richard III (History)
1593	Taming of the Shrew (Comedy) Titus Andronicus (Tragedy) Venus and Adonis (Poem)
1594	Rape of Lucrece (Poem) Romeo and Juliet (Tragedy) Two Gentlemen of Verona (Comedy) Love's Labour's Lost (Comedy)
1595	Richard II (History) Midsummer Night's Dream (Comedy)
1596	King John (History) Merchant of Venice (Comedy)
1597	Henry IV, Part I (History) Henry IV, Part II (History)
1598	Passionate Pilgrim (Poem) Henry V (History) Much Ado about Nothing (Comedy)
1599	Twelfth Night (Comedy) As You Like It (Comedy) Julius Caesar (Tragedy)
1600	Hamlet (Tragedy) Merry Wives of Windsor (Comedy)
1601	Troilus and Cressida (Comedy)
1601	Phoenix and the Turtle (Poem))
1602	All's Well That Ends Well (Comedy)
1604	Othello (Tragedy) Measure for Measure

1605	King Lear (Tragedy)
	Macbeth (Tragedy)
1606	Antony and Cleopatra (Tragedy)
1607	Coriolanus (Tragedy)
	Timon of Athens (Tragedy)
1608	Pericles (Comedy)
1609	Cymbeline (Comedy)
	Lover's Complaint (Poem)
1610	Winter's Tale (Comedy)
1611	Tempest (Comedy)
1612	Henry VIII (History)

As regards his 154 sonnets it is almost impossible to date each individually though collectively they were first published in 1609, with two having been published in 1599.

Shakspeare; or, the Poet by Ralph Waldo Emerson

Great (1) men are more distinguished by range and extent than by originality. If we require the originality which consists in weaving, like a spider, their web from their own bowels; in finding clay and making bricks and building the house; no great men are original. Nor does valuable originality consist in unlikeness to other men. The hero is in the press of knights and the thick of events; and seeing what men want and sharing their desire, he adds the needful length of sight and of arm, to come at the desired point. The greatest genius is the most indebted man. A poet is no rattle-brain, saying what comes uppermost, and, because he says every thing, saying at last something good; but a heart in unison with his time and country. There is nothing whimsical and fantastic in his production, but sweet and sad earnest, freighted with the weightiest convictions and pointed with the most determined aim which any man or class knows of in his times. (2)

The Genius of our life is jealous of individuals, and will not have any individual great, except through the general. There is no choice to genius. A great man does not wake up on some fine morning and say, 'I am full of life, I will go to sea and find an Antarctic continent: to-day I will square the circle: I will ransack botany and find a new food for man: I have a new architecture in my mind: I foresee a new mechanic power:' no, but he finds himself in the river of the thoughts and events, forced onward by the ideas and necessities of his contemporaries. (3) He stands where all the eyes of men look one way, and their hands all point in the direction in which he should go. The Church has reared him amidst rites and pomps, and he carries out the advice which her music gave him, and builds a cathedral needed by her chants and processions. He finds a war raging: it educates him, by trumpet, in barracks, and he betters the instruction. He finds two counties groping to bring coal, or flour, or fish, from the place of production to the place of consumption, and he hits on a railroad. Every master has found his materials collected, and his power lay in his sympathy with his people and in his love of the materials he wrought in. What an economy of power! and what a compensation for the shortness of life! All is done to his hand. The world has brought him thus far on his way. The human race has gone out before him, sunk the hills, filled the hollows and bridged the rivers. Men, nations, poets, artisans, women, all have worked for him, and he enters into their labors. Choose any other thing, out of the line of tendency, out of the national feeling and history, and he would have all to do for himself: his powers would be expended in the first preparations. Great genial power, one would almost say, consists in not being original at all; in being altogether receptive; in letting the world do all, and suffering the spirit of the hour to pass unobstructed through the mind. (4)

Shakspeare's youth fell in a time when the English people were importunate for dramatic entertainments. The court took offence easily at political allusions and attempted to suppress them. The Puritans, a growing and energetic party, and the religious among the Anglican church, would suppress them. But the people wanted them. Inn-yards, houses without roofs, and extemporaneous enclosures at country fairs were the ready theatres of strolling players. The people had tasted this new joy; and, as we could not hope to suppress newspapers now,—no, not by the strongest party,— neither then could king, prelate, or puritan, alone or united, suppress an organ which was ballad, epic, newspaper, caucus, lecture, Punch and library, at the same time. Probably king, prelate and puritan, all found their own account in it. It had become, by all causes, a national interest,—by no means conspicuous, so that some great scholar would have thought of treating it in an English history,—but not a whit less considerable because it was cheap and of no account, like a baker's-shop. The best proof of its vitality is the crowd of writers which suddenly broke into this field; Kyd, Marlow, Greene, Jonson, Chapman, Dekker, Webster, Heywood, Middleton, Peele, Ford, Massinger, Beaumont and Fletcher.

The secure possession, by the stage, of the public mind, is of the first importance to the poet who works for it. (5) He loses no time in idle experiments. Here is audience and expectation prepared. In the case of Shakspeare there is much more. At the time when he left Stratford and went up to London, a great body of stage-plays of all dates and writers existed in manuscript and were in turn produced on the boards. Here is the Tale of Troy, which the audience will bear hearing some part of, every week; the Death of Julius Cæsar, and other stories out of Plutarch, which they never tire of; a shelf full of English history, from the chronicles of Brut and Arthur, down to the royal Henries, which men hear eagerly; and a string of doleful tragedies, merry Italian tales and Spanish voyages, which all the London 'prentices know. All the mass has been treated, with more or less skill, by every playwright, and the prompter has the soiled and tattered manuscripts. It is now no longer possible to say who wrote them first. They have been the property of the Theatre so long, and so many rising geniuses have enlarged or altered them, inserting a speech or a whole scene, or adding a song, that no man can any longer claim copyright in this work of numbers. Happily, no man wishes to. They are not yet desired in that way. We have few readers, many spectators and hearers. They had best lie where they are.

Shakspeare, in common with his comrades, esteemed the mass of old plays waste stock, in which any experiment could be freely tried. Had the prestige which hedges about a modern tragedy existed, nothing could have been done. The rude warm blood of the living England circulated in the play, as in street-ballads, and gave body which he wanted to his airy and majestic fancy. The poet needs a ground in popular tradition on which he may work, and which, again, may restrain his art within the due temperance. It holds him to the people, supplies a foundation for his edifice, and in furnishing so much work done to his hand, leaves him at leisure and in full strength for the audacities of his imagination. In short, the poet owes to his legend what sculpture owed to the temple. Sculpture in Egypt and in Greece grew up in subordination to architecture. It was the ornament of the temple wall: at first a rude relief carved on pediments, then the relief became bolder and a head or arm was projected from the wall; the groups being still arranged with reference to the building, which serves also as a frame to hold the figures; and when at last the greatest freedom of style and treatment was reached, the prevailing genius of architecture still enforced a certain calmness and continence in the statue. As soon as the statue was begun for itself, and with no reference to the temple or palace, the art began to decline: freak, extravagance and exhibition took the place of the old temperance. This balance-wheel, which the sculptor found in architecture, the perilous irritability of poetic talent found in the accumulated dramatic materials to which the people were already wonted, and which had a certain excellence which no single genius, however extraordinary, could hope to create.

In point of fact it appears that Shakspeare did owe debts in all directions, and was able to use whatever he found; and the amount of indebtedness may be inferred from Malone's laborious computations in regard to the First, Second and Third parts of Henry VI., in which, "out of 6043 lines, 1771 were written by some author preceding Shakspeare, 2373 by him, on the foundation laid by his predecessors, and 1899 were entirely his own." And the proceeding investigation hardly leaves a single drama of his absolute invention. Malone's sentence is an important piece of external history. In Henry VIII. I think I see plainly the cropping out of the original rock on which his own finer stratum was laid. The first play was written by a superior, thoughtful man, with a vicious ear. I can mark his lines, and know well their cadence. See Wolsey's soliloquy, and the following scene with Cromwell, where instead of the metre of Shakspeare, whose secret is that the thought constructs the tune, so that reading for the sense will best bring out the rhythm,—here the lines are constructed on a given tune, and the verse has even a trace of pulpit eloquence. But the play contains through all its length unmistakable traits of Shakspeare's hand, and some passages, as the account of the coronation, are like autographs. What is odd, the compliment to Queen Elizabeth is in the bad rhythm. (6)

Shakspeare knew that tradition supplies a better fable than any invention can. If he lost any credit of design, he augmented his resources; and, at that day, our petulant demand for originality was not so much pressed. There was no literature for the million. The universal reading, the cheap press, were unknown. A great poet who appears in illiterate times, absorbs into his sphere all the light which is any where radiating. Every intellectual jewel, every flower of sentiment it is his fine office to bring to his people; and he comes to value his memory equally with his invention. (7) He is therefore little solicitous whence his thoughts have been derived; whether through translation, whether through tradition, whether by travel in distant countries, whether by inspiration; from whatever source, they are equally welcome to his uncritical audience. Nay, he borrows very near home. Other men say wise things as well as he; only they say a good many foolish things, and do not know when they have spoken wisely. He knows the sparkle of the true stone, and puts it in high place, wherever he finds it. (8) Such is the happy position of Homer perhaps; of Chaucer, of Saadi. They felt that all wit was their wit. And they are librarians and historiographers, as well as poets. Each romancer was heir and dispenser of all the hundred tales of the world,—

"Presenting Thebes' and Pelops' line
And the tale of Troy divine." (9)

The influence of Chaucer is conspicuous in all our early literature; and more recently not only Pope and Dryden have been beholden to him, but, in the whole society of English writers, a large unacknowledged debt is easily traced. One is charmed with the opulence which feeds so many pensioners. But Chaucer is a huge borrower. Chaucer, it seems, drew continually, through Lydgate and Caxton, from Guido di Colonna, whose Latin romance of the Trojan war was in turn a compilation from Dares Phrygius, Ovid and Statius. Then Petrarch, Boccaccio and the Provençal poets are his benefactors: the Romaunt of the Rose is only judicious translation from William of Lorris and John of Meung: Troilus and Creseide, from Lollius of Urbino: The Cock and the Fox, from the Lais of Marie: The House of Fame, from the French or Italian: and poor Gower he uses as if he were only a brick-kiln or stone-quarry out of which to build his house. (10) He steals by this apology,—that what he takes has no worth where he finds it and the greatest where he leaves it. It has come to be practically a sort of rule in literature, that a man having once shown himself capable of original writing, is entitled thenceforth to steal from the writings of others at discretion. Thought is the property of him who can entertain it and of him who can adequately place it. A certain awkwardness marks the use of borrowed thoughts; but as soon as we have learned what to do with them they become our own.

Thus all originality is relative. Every thinker is retrospective. The learned member of the legislature, at Westminster or at Washington, speaks and votes for thousands. Show us the constituency, and the now invisible channels by which the senator is made aware of their wishes; the crowd of practical and knowing men, who, by correspondence or conversation, are feeding him with evidence, anecdotes and estimates, and it will bereave his fine attitude and resistance of something of their impressiveness. As Sir Robert Peel and Mr. Webster vote, so Locke and Rousseau think, for thousands; and so there were fountains all around Homer, (11) Menu, Saadi, or Milton, from which they drew; friends, lovers, books, traditions, proverbs,—all perished—which, if seen, would go to reduce the wonder. Did the bard speak with authority? Did he feel himself overmatched by any companion? The appeal is to the consciousness of the writer. Is there at last in his breast a Delphi whereof to ask concerning any thought or thing, whether it be verily so, yea or nay? and to have answer, and to rely on that? All the debts which such a man could contract to other wit would never disturb his consciousness of originality; for the ministrations of books and of other minds are a whiff of smoke to that most private reality with which he has conversed. (12)

It is easy to see that what is best written or done by genius in the world, was no man's work, but came by wide social labor, when a thousand wrought like one, sharing the same impulse. Our English Bible is a wonderful specimen of the strength and music of the English language. But it was not made by one man, or at one time; but centuries and churches brought it to perfection. There never was a time when there was not some translation existing. The Liturgy, admired for its energy and pathos, is an anthology of the piety of ages and nations, a translation of the prayers and forms of the Catholic church,—these collected, too, in long periods, from the prayers and meditations of every saint and sacred writer all over the world. (13) Grotius makes the like remark in respect to the Lord's Prayer, that the single clauses of which it is composed were already in use in the time of Christ, in the Rabbinical forms. He picked out the grains of gold. The nervous language of the Common Law, the impressive forms of our courts and the precision and substantial truth of the legal distinctions, are the contribution of all the sharp-sighted, strong-minded men who have lived in the countries where these laws govern. The translation of Plutarch gets its excellence by being translation on translation. There never was a time when there was none. All the truly idiomatic and national phrases are kept, and all others successively picked out and thrown away. Something like the same process had gone on, long before, with the originals of these books. The world takes liberties with world-books. Vedas, Æsop's Fables, Pilpay, Arabian Nights, Cid, Iliad, Robin Hood, Scottish Minstrelsy, are not the work of single men. In the composition of such works the time thinks, the market thinks, the mason, the carpenter, the merchant, the farmer, the fop, all think for us. Every book supplies its time with one good word; every municipal law, every trade, every folly of the day; and the generic catholic genius who is not afraid or ashamed to owe his originality to the originality of all, stands with the next age as the recorder and embodiment of his own. (14)

We have to thank the researches of antiquaries, and the Shakspeare Society, for ascertaining the steps of the English drama, from the Mysteries celebrated in churches and by churchmen, and the final detachment from the church, and the completion of secular plays, from Ferrex and Porrex, (15) and Gammer Gurton's Needle, down to the possession of the stage by the very pieces which Shakspeare altered, remodelled and finally made his own. Elated with success and piqued by the growing interest of the problem, they have left no bookstall unsearched, no chest in a garret unopened, no file of old yellow accounts to decompose in damp and worms, so keen was the hope to discover whether the boy Shakspeare poached or not, whether he held horses at the theatre door, whether he kept school, and why he left in his will only his second-best bed to Ann Hathaway, his wife.

There is somewhat touching in the madness with which the passing age mischooses the object on which all candles shine and all eyes are turned; the care with which it registers every trifle touching Queen Elizabeth and King James, and the Essexes, Leicesters, Burleighs and Buckinghams; and lets pass without a single valuable note the founder of another dynasty, which alone will cause the Tudor dynasty to be remembered,—the man who carries the Saxon race in him by the inspiration which feeds him, and on whose thoughts the foremost people of the world are now for some ages to be nourished, and minds to receive this and not another bias. A popular player;—nobody suspected he was the poet of the human race; and the secret was kept as faithfully from poets and intellectual men as from courtiers and frivolous people. (16) Bacon, who took the inventory of the human understanding for his times, never mentioned his name. Ben Jonson, though we have strained his few words of regard and panegyric, had no suspicion of the elastic fame whose first vibrations he was attempting. He no doubt thought the praise he has conceded to him generous, and esteemed himself, out of all question, the better poet of the two.

If it need wit to know wit, according to the proverb, Shakspeare's time should be capable of recognizing it. Sir Henry Wotton was born four years after Shakspeare, and died twenty-three years after him; and I find, among his correspondents and acquaintances, the following persons: Theodore Beza, Isaac Casaubon, Sir Philip Sidney, the Earl of Essex, Lord Bacon, Sir Walter Raleigh, John Milton, Sir Henry Vane, Isaac Walton, Dr. Donne, Abraham Cowley, Bellarmine, Charles Cotton, John Pym, John Hales, Kepler, Vieta, Albericus Gentilis, Paul Sarpi, Arminius; with all of whom exists some token of his having communicated, without enumerating many others whom doubtless he saw,— Shakspeare, Spenser, Jonson, Beaumont, Massinger, the two Herberts, Marlow, Chapman and the rest. Since the constellation of great men who appeared in Greece in the time of Pericles, there was never any such society;—yet their genius failed them to find out the best head in the universe. (17) Our poet's mask was impenetrable. You cannot see the mountain near. It took a century to make it suspected; and not until two centuries had passed, after his death, did any criticism which we think adequate begin to appear. It was not possible to write the history of Shakspeare till now; for he is the father of German literature: it was with the introduction of Shakspeare into German, by Lessing, and the translation of his works by Wieland and Schlegel, that the rapid burst of German literature was most intimately connected. It was not until the nineteenth century, whose speculative genius is a sort of living Hamlet, that the tragedy of Hamlet could find such wondering readers. (18) Now, literature, philosophy and thought are Shakspearized. His mind is the horizon beyond which, at present, we do not see. Our ears are educated to music by his rhythm. Coleridge and Goethe are the only critics who have expressed our convictions with any adequate fidelity: but there is in all cultivated minds a silent appreciation of his superlative power and beauty, which, like Christianity, qualifies the period.

The Shakspeare Society have inquired in all directions, advertised the missing facts, offered money for any information that will lead to proof,—and with what result? Beside some important illustration of the history of the English stage, to which I have adverted, they have gleaned a few facts touching the property, and dealings in regard to property, of the poet. It appears that from year to year he owned a larger share in the Blackfriars' Theatre: its wardrobe and other appurtenances were his: that he bought an estate in his native village with his earnings as writer and shareholder; that he lived in the best house in Stratford; was intrusted by his neighbors with their commissions in London, as of borrowing money, and the like; that he was a veritable farmer. About the time when he was writing Macbeth, he sues Philip Rogers, in the borough-court of Stratford, for thirty-five shillings, ten pence, for corn delivered to him at different times; and in all respects appears as a good husband, with no reputation for eccentricity or excess. He was a good-natured sort of man, an actor and shareholder in the theatre, not in any striking manner distinguished from other actors and managers. (19) I admit the importance of this information. It was well worth the pains that have been taken to procure it.

But whatever scraps of information concerning his condition these researches may have rescued, they can shed no light upon that infinite invention which is the concealed magnet of his attraction for us. We are very clumsy writers of history. We tell the chronicle of parentage, birth, birth-place, schooling, school-mates, earning of money, marriage, publication of books, celebrity, death; and when we have come to an end of this gossip, no ray of relation appears between it and the goddess-born; and it seems as if, had we dipped at random into the "Modern Plutarch," and read any other life there, it would have fitted the poems as well. (20) It is the essence of poetry to spring, like the rainbow daughter of Wonder, from the invisible, to abolish the past and refuse all history. Malone, Warburton, Dyce and Collier have wasted their oil. The famed theatres, Covent Garden, Drury Lane, the Park and Tremont have vainly assisted. Betterton, Garrick, Kemble, Kean and Macready dedicate their lives to this genius; him they crown, elucidate, obey and express. The genius knows them not. The recitation begins; one golden word leaps out immortal from all this painted pedantry and sweetly torments us with invitations to its own inaccessible homes. I remember I went once to see the Hamlet of a famed performer, the pride of the English stage; and all I then heard and all I now remember of the tragedian was that in which the tragedian had no part; simply Hamlet's question to the ghost:—

"What may this mean,
That thou, dead corse, again in complete steel
Revisit'st thus the glimpses of the moon?"

That imagination which dilates the closet he writes in to the world's dimension, crowds it with agents in rank and order, as quickly reduces the big reality to be the glimpses of the moon. (21) These tricks of his magic spoil for us the illusions of the green-room. Can any biography shed light on the localities into which the Midsummer Night's Dream admits me? Did Shakspeare confide to any notary or parish recorder, sacristan, or surrogate in Stratford, the genesis of that delicate creation? The forest of Arden, the nimble air of Scone Castle, the moonlight of Portia's villa, "the antres vast and desarts idle" of Othello's captivity,—where is the third cousin, or grand-nephew, the chancellor's file of accounts, or private letter, that has kept one word of those transcendent secrets? In fine, in this drama, as in all great works of art,—in the Cyclopæan architecture of Egypt and India, in the Phidian sculpture, the Gothic minsters, the Italian painting, the Ballads of Spain and Scotland,—the Genius draws up the ladder after him, when the creative age goes up to heaven, and gives way to a new age, which sees the works and asks in vain for a history.

Shakspeare is the only biographer of Shakspeare; and even he can tell nothing, except to the Shakspeare in us, that is, to our most apprehensive and sympathetic hour. (22) He cannot step from off his tripod and give us anecdotes of his inspirations. Read the antique documents extricated, analyzed and compared by the assiduous Dyce and Collier, and now read one of these skyey sentences,—aerolites,—which seem to have fallen out of heaven, and which not your experience but the man within the breast has accepted as words of fate, and tell me if they match; if the former account in any manner for the latter; or which gives the most historical insight into the man.

Hence, though our external history is so meagre, yet, with Shakspeare for biographer, instead of Aubrey and Rowe, we have really the information which is material; that which describes character and fortune, that which, if we were about to meet the man and deal with him, would most import us to know. We have his recorded convictions on those questions which knock for answer at every heart,—on life and death, on love, on wealth and poverty, on the prizes of life and the ways whereby we come at them; on the characters of men, and the influences, occult and open, which affect their fortunes; and on those mysterious and demoniacal powers which defy our science and which yet interweave their malice and their gift in our brightest hours. Who ever read the volume of the Sonnets without finding that the poet had there revealed, under masks that are no masks to the intelligent, the lore of friendship and of love; the confusion of sentiments in the most susceptible, and, at the same time, the most intellectual of men? What trait of his private mind has he hidden in his dramas? One can discern, in his ample pictures of the gentleman and the king, what forms and humanities pleased him; his delight in troops of friends, in large hospitality, in cheerful giving. Let Timon, let Warwick, let Antonio the merchant answer for his great heart. So far from Shakspeare's being the least known, he is the one person, in all modern history, known to us. What point of morals, of manners, of economy, of philosophy, of religion, of taste, of the conduct of life, has he not settled? What mystery has he not signified his knowledge of? What office, or function, or district of man's work, has he not remembered? What king has he not taught state, as Talma taught Napoleon? What maiden has not found him finer than her delicacy? What lover has he not outloved? What sage has he not outseen? What gentleman has he not instructed in the rudeness of his behavior?

Some able and appreciating critics think no criticism on Shakspeare valuable that does not rest purely on the dramatic merit; that he is falsely judged as poet and philosopher. I think as highly as these critics of his dramatic merit, but still think it secondary. He was a full man, who liked to talk; a brain exhaling thoughts and images, which, seeking vent, found the drama next at hand. (23) Had he been less, we should have had to consider how well he filled his place, how good a dramatist he was,—and he is the best in the world. But it turns out that what he has to say is of that weight as to withdraw some attention from the vehicle; and he is like some saint whose history is to be rendered into all languages, into verse and prose, into songs and pictures, and cut up into proverbs; so that the occasion which gave the saint's meaning the form of a conversation, or of a prayer, or of a code of laws, is immaterial compared with the universality of its application. So it fares with the wise Shakspeare and his book of life. He wrote the airs for all our modern music: he wrote the text of modern life; the text of manners: he drew the man of England and Europe; the father of the man in America; (24) he drew the man, and described the day, and what is done in it: he read the hearts of men and women, their probity, and their second thought and wiles; the wiles of innocence, and the transitions by which virtues and vices slide into their contraries: he could divide the mother's part from the father's part in the face of the child, or draw the fine demarcations of freedom and of fate: he knew the laws of repression which make the police of nature: and all the sweets and all the terrors of human lot lay in his mind as truly but as softly as the landscape lies on the eye. And the importance of this wisdom of life sinks the form, as of Drama or Epic, out of notice. 'T is like making a question concerning the paper on which a king's message is written.

Shakspeare is as much out of the category of eminent authors, as he is out of the crowd. He is inconceivably wise; the others, conceivably. A good reader can, in a sort, nestle into Plato's brain and think from thence; but not into Shakspeare's. We are still out of doors. For executive faculty, for creation, Shakspeare is unique. No man can imagine it better. He was the farthest reach of subtlety compatible with an individual self,—the subtilest of authors, and only just within the possibility of authorship. (25) With this wisdom of life is the equal endowment of imaginative and of lyric power. He clothed the creatures of his legend with form and sentiments as if they were people who had lived under his roof; and few real men have left such distinct characters as these fictions. And they spoke in language as sweet as it was fit. Yet his talents never seduced him into an ostentation, nor did he harp on one string. An omnipresent humanity co-ordinates all his faculties. Give a man of talents a story to tell, and his partiality will presently appear. He has certain observations, opinions, topics, which have some accidental prominence, and which he disposes all to exhibit. He crams this part and starves that other part, consulting not the fitness of the thing, but his fitness and strength. But Shakspeare has no peculiarity, no importunate topic; but all is duly given; no veins, no curiosities; no cow-painter, no bird-fancier, no mannerist is he: he has no discoverable egotism: the great he tells greatly; the small subordinately. He is wise without emphasis or assertion; he is strong, as nature is strong, who lifts the land into mountain slopes without effort and by the same rule as she floats a bubble in the air, and likes as well to do the one as the other. This makes that equality of power in farce, tragedy, narrative, and love-songs; a merit so incessant that each reader is incredulous of the perception of other readers.

This power of expression, or of transferring the inmost truth of things into music and verse, makes him the type of the poet and has added a new problem to metaphysics. This is that which throws him into natural history, as a main production of the globe, and as announcing new eras and ameliorations. Things were mirrored in his poetry without loss or blur: he could paint the fine with precision, the great with compass, the tragic and the comic indifferently and without any distortion or favor. He carried his powerful execution into minute details, to a hair point; finishes an eyelash or a dimple as firmly as he draws a mountain; and yet these, like nature's, will bear the scrutiny of the solar microscope.

In short, he is the chief example to prove that more or less of production, more or fewer pictures, is a thing indifferent. He had the power to make one picture. Daguerre learned how to let one flower etch its image on his plate of iodine, and then proceeds at leisure to etch a million. There are always objects; but there was never representation. Here is perfect representation, at last; and now let the world of figures sit for their portraits. No recipe can be given for the making of a Shakspeare; but the possibility of the translation of things into song is demonstrated.

His lyric power lies in the genius of the piece. The sonnets, though their excellence is lost in the splendor of the dramas, are as inimitable as they; and it is not a merit of lines, but a total merit of the piece; like the tone of voice of some incomparable person, so is this speech of poetic beings, and any clause as unproducible now as a whole poem.

Though the speeches in the plays, and single lines, have a beauty which tempts the ear to pause on them for their euphuism, yet the sentence is so loaded with meaning and so linked with its foregoers and followers, that the logician is satisfied. His means are as admirable as his ends; every subordinate invention, by which he helps himself to connect some irreconcilable opposites, is a poem too. He is not reduced to dismount and walk because his horses are running off with him in some distant direction: he always rides.
The finest poetry was first experience; but the thought has suffered a transformation since it was an experience. Cultivated men often attain a good degree of skill in writing verses; but it is easy to read, through their poems, their personal history: any one acquainted with the parties can name every figure; this is Andrew and that is Rachel. The sense thus remains prosaic. It is a caterpillar with wings, and not yet a butterfly. In the poet's mind the fact has gone quite over into the new element of thought, and has lost all that is exuvial. This generosity abides with Shakespeare. We say, from the truth and closeness of his pictures, that he knows the lesson by heart. Yet there is not a trace of egotism.

One more royal trait properly belongs to the poet. I mean his cheerfulness, without which no man can be a poet,—for beauty is his aim. He loves virtue, not for its obligation but for its grace: he delights in the world, in man, in woman, for the lovely light that sparkles from them. Beauty, the spirit of joy and hilarity, he sheds over the universe. Epicurus relates that poetry hath such charms that a lover might forsake his mistress to partake of them. And the true bards have been noted for their firm and cheerful temper. Homer lies in sunshine; Chaucer is glad and erect; and Saadi says, "It was rumored abroad that I was penitent; but what had I to do with repentance?" (26) Not less sovereign and cheerful,—much more sovereign and cheerful, is the tone of Shakespeare. His name suggests joy and emancipation to the heart of men. If he should appear in any company of human souls, who would not march in his troop? He touches nothing that does not borrow health and longevity from his festal style.

And now, how stands the account of man with this bard and benefactor, when, in solitude, shutting our ears to the reverberations of his fame, we seek to strike the balance? Solitude has austere lessons; it can teach us to spare both heroes and poets; and it weighs Shakespeare also, and finds him to share the halfness and imperfection of humanity.

Shakespeare, Homer, Dante, Chaucer, saw the splendor of meaning that plays over the visible world; knew that a tree had another use than for apples, and corn another than for meal, and the ball of the earth, than for tillage and roads: that these things bore a second and finer harvest to the mind, being emblems of its thoughts, and conveying in all their natural history a certain mute commentary on human life. (27) Shakespeare employed them as colors to compose his picture. He rested in their beauty; and never took the step which seemed inevitable to such genius, namely to explore the virtue which resides in these symbols and imparts this power:—what is that which they themselves say? He converted the elements which waited on his command, into entertainments. He was master of the revels to mankind. Is it not as if one should have, through majestic powers of science, the comets given into his hand, or the planets and their moons, and should draw them from their orbits to glare with the municipal fireworks on a holiday night, and advertise in all towns, "Very superior pyrotechny this evening"? Are the agents of nature, and the power to understand them, worth no more than a street serenade, or the breath of a cigar? One remembers again the trumpet-text in the Koran,—"The heavens and the earth and all that is between them, think ye we have created them in jest?" As long as the question is of talent and mental power, the world of men has not his equal to show. But when the question is, to life and its materials and its auxiliaries, how does he profit me? What does it signify? It is but a Twelfth Night, or Midsummer-Night's Dream, or Winter Evening's Tale: what signifies another picture more or less? The Egyptian verdict of the Shakespeare Societies comes to mind; that he was a jovial actor and manager. I can not marry this fact to his verse. Other admirable men have led lives in some sort of keeping with their thought; but this man, in wide contrast. Had he been less, had he reached only the common measure of great authors, of Bacon, Milton, Tasso, Cervantes, we might leave the fact in the twilight of human fate: but that this man of men, he who gave to the science of mind a new and larger subject than had ever existed, and planted the standard of humanity some furlongs forward into Chaos,—that he should not be wise for himself;—it must even go into the world's history that the best poet led an obscure and profane life, using his genius for the public amusement. (28)

Well, other men, priest and prophet, Israelite, German and Swede, beheld the same objects: they also saw through them that which was contained. And to what purpose? The beauty straightway vanished; they read commandments, all-excluding mountainous duty; an obligation, a sadness, as of piled mountains, fell on them, and life became ghastly, joyless, a pilgrim's progress, a probation, beleaguered round with doleful histories of Adam's fall and curse behind us; with doomsdays and purgatorial and penal fires before us; and the heart of the seer and the heart of the listener sank in them.

It must be conceded that these are half-views of half-men. The world still wants its poet-priest, a reconciler, who shall not trifle, with Shakespeare the player, nor shall grope in graves, with Swedenborg the mourner; but who shall see, speak, and act, with equal inspiration. For knowledge will brighten the sunshine; right is more beautiful than private affection; and love is compatible with universal wisdom. (29)

Footnotes

Note 1.

This essay was read as a lecture in Exeter Hall, in London, in June, 1848.

Perhaps it is well to bear in mind that Mr. Emerson was reared for the ministry and ordained a clergyman, and that his ancestors for several generations had exercised that office, and moreover that, in New England, up to his day, theatrical representations had been looked at with disfavor by serious and God-fearing people, and the witnessing of such by a minister would, like dancing, have been considered unbecoming indulgence. Although Mr. Emerson emancipated himself from bonds that were merely professional or artificial, he had an inbred distaste for the common amusements of society, feeling that they were unbecoming to a scholar, and that he was not adapted for them, though he was tolerant of them in other people. There was a natural earnestness, and a simple and cheerful asceticism in his early and later life. Yet once in his later life, when he had been induced to go to see Mr. and Mrs. Barney Williams in some bright comedy, he praised their acting and admitted to his daughter that he really much enjoyed theatrical performances, in spite of the feeling that they were not for him. Dancing, for instance, which he considered a proper part of youths' education, would have seemed unbecoming for himself. He says, "It shall be writ in my memoirs ... as it was writ of St. Pachonius, Pes ejus ad saltandum non est commotus omni vita sua." His staying away from theatrical entertainments was instinctive, but he was liberal in the matter and would go to see a real artist. He even went to see the performance of the beautiful dancer Fanny Elssler, although a story which has been too often repeated of his remarks to Margaret Fuller on the subject is as false as it is silly.

In Paris he saw Rachel during the Revolution of 1848, and often told his children of her fierce and splendid declamation of the Marseillaise in the theatre, holding the tricolor aloft. On London in that same year he wrote of seeing Macready in Lear, with Mrs. Butler as Cordelia. It was to see one of Shakspeare's heroes rendered by some master that he went, and probably he never was inside a theatre twenty times in his life, and, so sensitive was he to had taste or ranting, that he was usually sorry that had gone.

The rendering of Richard II. (I cannot remember by whom) more than satisfied him, and he liked to recall the actor's tones in reading this play, an especial favorite of his, to his children. Coriolanus and Julius Cæsar too he enjoyed reading to them, and he selected passages from Shakspeare for them and trained them very carefully for their recitation in school.

He saw Edwin Booth in Boston, and met him later at the house of a friend and had some talk with him. Booth later mentioned with pleasure to their host the fact that Mr. Emerson had not once alluded to his profession or performance in their conversation.

Mr. Emerson once defined the cultivated man as "one who can tell you something new and true about Shakspeare." And he read a good omen for our age in Shakspeare's acceptance: "The book only characterizes the reader. Is Shakspeare the delight of the nineteenth century? That fact only shows whereabouts we are in the ecliptic of the soul."

In writing of Great Men in 1838 in his journal, he says:—

"Swedenborg is scarce yet appreciable. Shakspeare has, for the first time, in our time found adequate criticism, if indeed he have yet found it:—Coleridge, Lamb, Schlegel, Goethe, Very, Herder.

"The great facts of history are four or five names, Homer—Phidias—Jesus—Shakspeare. One or two names more I will not add, but see what these names stand for. All civil history and all philosophy consists of endeavours more or less vain to explain these persons."

In the journal for 1843 he writes: "Plato is weak inasmuch as he is literary. Shakspeare is not literary, but the strong earth itself." Yet from another point of view he writes, "Shakspeare and Plato each sufficed for the culture of a nation."

That Shakspeare and Milton should have been born meant much to him and to mankind. "Who saw Milton, who saw Shakspeare, saw them do their best, and utter their whole heart manlike among their contemporaries."

And again, "No man can be named whose mind still acts on the cultivated intellect of England and America with an energy comparable to that of Milton. As a poet, Shakspeare undoubtedly transcends and far surpasses him in his popularity with foreign nations: but Shakspeare is a voice merely: who and what he was that sang, that sings, we know not."

Note 2.

Mr. Emerson said of Nature:—

No ray is dimmed, no atom worn,
My oldest force is good as new,
And the fresh rose on yonder thorn
Gives back the bending heavens in dew;—

and her cheerful lesson for the artist or poet was that he too could forever re-combine the old material into fresh and splendid pictures. He rejoiced that "the poet is permitted to dip his brush into the old paint-pot with which birds, flowers, the human cheek, the living rock, the broad landscape, the ocean and the eternal sky were painted," and turning from the reading of the plays he says: "'T is Shakspeare's fault that the world appears so empty. He has educated you with his painted world, and this real one seems a huckster's-shop." Again as to his true rendering of men's characters, "I value Shakspeare as a metaphysician and admire the unspoken logic which upholds the structure of Iago, Macbeth, Antony and the rest."

Note 3.

Again the ancient doctrine of the Flowing, and the modern onward and upward stream of Evolution.

Note 4.

The passive Master lent his hand
To the vast soul that o'er him planned.
"The Problem," Poems.

Note 5.

The stage was to Shakspeare his opportunity, as the Lyceum was to Emerson.

Note 6.

Henry VIII., Act V., Scene iv.

Note 7.

This estimate of the value of memory to the poet, typified by the Greeks in their making the Muses the daughters of Mnemosyne, is enlarged upon in the Essay on "Memory" in *Natural History of Intellect*. Mr. Emerson said once, "Of the most romantic fact the memory is more romantic," and he quotes Quintilian as saying, *Quantum ingenii, tantum memoriæ*.

Note 8.

In a fragment of verse written in Mr. Emerson's journal of 1831 on the yearning of the poet to enrich himself from the Treasury of the Universe, he says:—

And if to me it is not given
To fetch one ingot thence
Of that unfading gold of Heaven
His merchants may dispense,
Yet well I know the royal mine,

And know the sparkle of its ore,
Know Heaven's truth from lies that shine,—

Explored, they teach us to explore.
"Fragments on the Poet," *Poems*, Appendix.

Note 9.

Milton, "Il Penseroso."

Note 10.

Taine, in his *History of English Literature*, thus justifies Chaucer's borrowing or rendering:—

"Chaucer was capable of seeking out, in the old common forest of the middle ages, stories and legends, to replant them in his own soil and make them send out new shoots…. He has the right and power of copying and translating because by dint of retouching he impresses … his original mark. He re-creates what he imitates…. At the distance of a century and a half he has affinity with the poets of Elizabeth by his gallery of pictures."

The dates of Lydgate and Caxton show a mistake as to his use of them. Caxton, following Chaucer, when he introduced the printing-press to England, printed his poems and those of Lydgate, who was younger than Chaucer. In his *House of Fame*, Chaucer places, in his vision, "on a pillar higher than the rest, Homer and Livy, Dares the Phrygian, Guido Colonna, Geoffrey of Monmouth and the other historians of the war of Troy" [Taine's *History of English Literature*], a due recognition of his debt for Troylus and Cryseyde. As for Gower, he was Chaucer's exact contemporary and friend, and Chaucer dedicated this poem to him.

Note 11.

Kipling irreverently tells of Homer's borrowings thus:—

"When 'Omer smote 'is bloomin' lyre,
He 'd 'eard men sing by land an' sea;
An' what he thought 'e might require,
'E went an' took—the same as me!"
And says of his humble audience:—

"They knew 'e stole; 'e knew they knowed.
They did n't tell, nor make a fuss,
But winked at 'Omer down the road,
An' 'e winked back—the same as us!"

Note 12.

Dr. Holmes's remark with regard to the preceding page is: "The reason why Emerson has so much to say on this subject of borrowing, especially when treating of Plato and Shakspeare, is obvious enough. He was arguing his own cause—not defending himself," etc. In Letters and Social Aims, Mr. Emerson discusses Quotation and Originality.

Note 13.

Mr. Emerson had tender associations with the Book of Common Prayer. His mother had been brought up in the Episcopal communion, and the prayer-book of her youth was always by her, though after her marriage she attended her husband's church. [In Mr. Cabot's Memoir, vol. ii. p. 572, see Mr. Emerson's letter on his mother's death.]

Note 14.

Landor says of these borrowings of Shakspeare, "He breathed upon dead bodies and brought them to life."

Note 15.

The princes Ferrex and Porrex, brothers and rivals for the ancient British throne, are characters in the tragedy Gorboduc by Norton and Sackville, to which the date 1561 is assigned. Gammer Gurton's Needle is a comedy of the same period.

Note 16.

Journal, 1864. "Shakspeare puts us all out. No theory will account for him. He neglected his works, perchance he did not know their value? Ay, but he did; witness the sonnets. He went into company as a listener, hiding himself, [Greek]; was only remembered by all as a delightful companion."

Note 17.

England's genius filled all measure
Of heart and soul, of strength and pleasure,
Gave to the mind its emperor,

And life was larger than before:
Nor sequent centuries could hit
Orbit and sum of Shakspeare's wit.
The men who lived with him became
Poets, for the air was fame.
"The Solution," Poems.

Note 18.

While writing this, Mr. Emerson was surrounded by persons paralyzed for active life in the common world by the doubts of conscience or entangled in over-fine-spun webs of their intellect. [back]

Note 19.

Journal, 1837. "I either read or inferred to-day in the Westminster Review that Shakspeare was not a popular man in his day. How true and wise. He sat alone and walked alone, a visionary poet, and came with his piece, modest but discerning, to the players, and was too glad to get it received, whilst he was too superior not to see its transcendent claims."

Note 20.

The following is the "Exordium of a lecture on Poetry and Eloquence," given in London in 1848:

"Shakspeare is nothing but a large utterance. We cannot find that anything in his age was more worth telling than anything in ours; nor give any account of his existence, but only the fact that there was a wonderful symbolizer and expresser, who has no rival in the ages, and who has thrown an accidental lustre over his time and subject."

In the lecture on "Works and Days" he wrote, "Shakspeare made his Hamlet as a bird weaves its nest." And in that on "Inspiration" in Letters and Social Aims: "Shakspeare seems to you miraculous, but the wonderful juxtapositions, parallelisms, transfers, which his genius effected, were all to him locked together as links of a chain, and the mode precisely as conceivable and familiar to higher intelligence as the index-making of the literary hack."

Journal, 1838. "Read Lear yesterday and Hamlet to-day with new wonder and mused much on the great Soul in the broad continuous daylight of these poems. Especially I wonder at the perfect reception this wit and immense knowledge of life and intellectual superiority find in us all in connection with our utter incapacity to produce anything like it. The superior tone of Hamlet in all the conversations how perfectly preserved, without any mediocrity, much less any dulness in the other speakers.

"How real the loftiness! an inborn gentleman; and above that, an exalted intellect. What incessant growth and plenitude of thought,—pausing on itself never an instant, and each sally of wit sufficient to save the play. How true then and unerring the earnest of the dialogue, as when Hamlet talks with the Queen. How terrible his discourse! What less can be said of the perfect mastery, as by a superior being, of the conduct of the drama, as the free introduction of this capital advice to the players; the commanding good sense which never retreats except before the Godhead which inspires certain passages—the more I think of it, the more I wonder. I will think nothing impossible to man. No Parthenon, no sculpture, no picture, no architecture can be named beside this. All this is perfectly visible to me and to many,—the wonderful truth and mastery of this work, of these works,—yet for our lives could not I, or any man, or all men, produce anything comparable to one scene in Hamlet or

Lear. With all my admiration of this life-like picture, set me to producing a match for it, and I should instantly depart into mouthing rhetoric.... One other fact Shakspeare presents us; that not by books are great poets made. Somewhat—and much, he unquestionably owes to his books; but you could not find in his circumstances the history of his poems. It was made without hands in his invisible world. A mightier magic than any learning, the deep logic of cause and effect he studied: its roots were cast so deep, therefore it flung out its branches so high."

Note 21.

Mr. Edwin P. Whipple, writing in Harper's Monthly in 1882, relates how in a long drive with Mr. Emerson, after a lecture, "The conversation at last drifted to contemporary actors who assumed to personate leading characters in Shakspeare's greatest plays. Had I ever seen an actor who satisfied me when he pretended to be Hamlet or Othello, Lear or Macbeth? Yes, I had seen the elder Booth in these characters. Though not perfect, he approached nearer to perfection than any other actor I knew—

"'Ah,' said Emerson, [after] the three minutes I consumed in eulogizing Booth,... 'I see you are one of the happy mortals who are capable of being carried away by an actor of Shakspeare. Now, whenever I visit the theatre to witness the performance of one of his dramas, I am carried away by the poet. I went last Tuesday to see Macready in Hamlet. I got along very well until he came to the passage:—

"thou, dead corse, again, in complete steel,
Revisit'st thus the glimpses of the moon:"—

and then actor, theatre, all vanished in view of that solving and dissolving imagination, which could reduce this big globe and all it inherits into mere "glimpses of the moon." The play went on, but, absorbed in this one thought of the mighty master, I paid no heed to it.'

"What specially impressed me, as Emerson was speaking, was his glance at our surroundings as he slowly uttered, 'glimpses of the moon,' for here above us was the same moon which must have given birth to Shakspeare's thought.... Afterward, in his lecture on Shakspeare, Emerson made use of the thought suggested in our ride by moonlight. He said, 'That imagination which dilates the closet he writes in to the world's dimensions, crowds it with agents in rank and order, as quickly reduces the big reality to be the "glimpses of the moon."'... In the printed lecture, there is one sentence declaring the absolute insufficiency of any actor, in any theatre, to fix attention on himself while uttering Shakspeare's words, which seems to me the most exquisite statement ever made of the magical suggestiveness of Shakspeare's expression. I have often quoted it, but it will bear quotation again and again, as the best prose sentence ever written on this side of the Atlantic: 'The recitation begins; one golden word leaps out immortal from all this painted pedantry, and sweetly torments us with invitations to its own inaccessible homes.'"

Note 22.

The little Shakspeare in the maiden's heart
Makes Romeo of a ploughboy on his cart;
Opens the eye to Virtue's starlike meed
And gives persuasion to a gentle deed.
"The Enchanter," Poems, Appendix.

Note 23.

And yet perhaps there is some truth in Dr. Richard Garnett's word in his Life of Emerson:

"Emerson is incapable of contemplating Shakspeare with the eye of a dramatic critic."

Just after Mr. Emerson settled in Concord he read with great pleasure Henry Taylor's play Philip van Artevelde, then recently published. He wrote in his journal for 1835:—

"I think Taylor's poem is the best light we have ever had upon the genius of Shakspeare. We have made a miracle of Shakspeare, a haze of light instead of a guiding torch, by accepting unquestioned all the tavern stories about his want of education, and total unconsciousness. The internal evidence all the time is irresistible that he was no such person. He was a man, like this Taylor, of strong sense and of great cultivation; an excellent Latin scholar, and of extensive and select reading, so as to have formed his theories of many historical characters with as much clearness as Gibbon or Niebuhr or Goethe. He wrote for intelligent persons, and wrote with intention. He had Taylor's strong good sense, and added to it his own wonderful facility of execution which aerates and sublimes all language the moment he uses it, or more truly, animates every word."

Note 24.

Lowell, in one of his essays, calls attention to the survival in New England of the type of face of the English in Queen Elizabeth's day even more than in the mother country, and also to the old English expressions, obsolete in England, but still current on New England farms.

Note 25.

Journal, 1838. fills us with wonder the first time we approach him. We go away, and work and think, for years, and come again,—he astonishes us anew. Then, having drank deeply and saturated us with his genius, we lose sight of him for another period of years. By and by we return, and there he stands immeasurable as at first. We have grown wiser, but only that we should see him wiser than ever. He resembles a high mountain which the traveller sees in the morning, and thinks he shall quickly near it and pass it, and leave it behind. But he journeys all day till noon, till night. There still is the dim mountain close by him, having scarce altered its bearings since the morning light."

Note 26.

And yet it seemeth not to me
That the high gods love tragedy;
For Saadi sat in the sun,
And thanks was his contrition;

And yet his runes he rightly read,
And to his folk his message sped.
"Saadi," Poems.

Note 27.

This image appears in "The Apology" in the Poems.

Note 28.

The Puritan shrinking from the form in which the great poet embodied his thought or oracles or dreams still appears in the journal of 1852, yet, contrasted to the dismal seers, Shakspeare is well-nigh pardoned his levity.

"There was never anything more excellent came from a human brain than the plays of Shakspeare, bating only that they were plays. The Greek has a real advantage of them in the degree in which his dramas had a religious office. Could the priest look him in the face without blenching?"

In 1839 Mr. Emerson had written:—

"It is in the nature of things that the highest originality must be moral. The only person who can be entirely independent of this fountain of literature and equal to it, must be a prophet in his own proper person. Shakspeare, the first literary genius of the world, leans on the Bible: his poetry supposes it. If we examine this brilliant influence, Shakspeare, as it lies in our minds, we shall find it reverent, deeply indebted to the traditional morality, in short, compared with the tone of the prophets, Secondary. On the other hand, the Prophets do not imply the existence of Shakspeare or Homer,—to no books or arts,—only to dread Ideas and emotions."

Note 29.

All through his life Mr. Emerson felt increasing thankfulness for "the Spirit of joy which Shakspeare had shed over the Universe." In 1864 he wrote:—

"When I read Shakspeare, as lately, I think the criticism and study of him to be in their infancy. The wonder grows of his long obscurity:—how could you hide the only man that ever wrote from all men who delight in reading?"

And again he wrote: "Your criticism is profane. Shakspeare by Shakspeare. The poet in his interlunation is a critic,"—that is, his worst is criticised by his best performance.

Journal, 1864. "How to say it I know not, but I know that the point of praise of Shakspeare is the pure poetic power: he is the chosen closet companion, who can, at any moment, by incessant surprises, work the miracle of mythologizing every fact of the common life; as snow, or moonlight, or the level rays of sunrise lend a momentary glow to Pump and wood-pile."

And again: 1836. "It is easy to solve the problem of individual existence. Why Milton, Shakspeare, or Canova should be there is reason enough. But why the million should exist drunk with the opium of Time and Custom does not appear."

But even Shakspeare must not be idolized. The soul must rely on itself, that is, on the universal fountain of beauty, wisdom and goodness to which it is open. So thus he draws the moral:—

1838. "The indisposition of men to go back to the source and mix with Deity is the reason of degradation and decay. Education is expended in the measurement and imitation of effects in the study of Shakspeare, for example, as itself a perfect being—instead of using Shakspeare merely as an effect of which the cause is with every scholar. Thus the college becomes idolatrous—a temple full of idols. Shakspeare will never be made by the study of Shakspeare. I know not how directions for greatness can be given, yet greatness may be inspired."

Feb. 1838. "Consider too how Shakspeare and Milton are formed. They are just such men as we all are to contemporaries, and none suspected their superiority,—but after all were dead, and a generation or two besides, it is discovered that they surpass all. Each of us then take the same moral to himself."

William Shakespeare – A Tribute in Verse

Index of Contents
To the Memory of My Beloved, the Author, Mr William Shakespeare, & What He Hath Left Us by Ben Jonson
Shakespeare by Matthew Arnold
An Epitaph On The Admirable Dramatic Poet W. Shakespeare by John Milton
Shakespeare by Henry Wadsworth Longfellow
Elegy On Mr. William Shakespeare by William Basse
Shakespeare by Vachel Lindsay
The Spirit of Shakespeare by George Meredith
To Shakespeare by Lord Alfred Douglas
To Shakespeare (I) by Frances Anne Kemble
To Shakespeare (II) by Frances Anne Kemble
To Shakespeare (III) by Frances Anne Kemble
Shakespeare and Milton by Walter Savage Landor
A Shakespeare Memorial by Alfred Austin
Shakespeare by Mathilde Blind
Shakespeare by Robert Crawford
Shakespeare by Thomas Gent
Shakespeare's Mourners by John Bannister Tabb
Shakespeare by Philip Henry Savage
Shakespeare by Lucretia Maria Davidson
Shakespeare by Frederick George Scott
Shakespeare's Kingdom by Alfred Noyes
Shakespeare 1916 by Sir Ronald Ross
Song, In Imitation of Shakspeare's by James Beattie
In A Letter To C. P. Esq. In Imitation o Shakspeare by William Cowper
Shakspeare. (An Ode For His Three-Hundredth Birthday) by Martin Farquhar Tupper
On The Site of A Mulberry-Tree; Planted By Wm. Shakspeare; Felled By The Rev. F. Gastrell by Dante Gabriel Rossetti

To The Memory of My Beloved, The Author, Mr William Shakespeare, And What He Hath Left Us by Ben Jonson

To draw no envy, Shakespeare, on thy name
Am I thus ample to thy book and fame;
While I confess thy writings to be such
As neither Man nor Muse can praise too much.
'Tis true, and all men's suffrage. But these ways
Were not the paths I meant unto thy praise;
For silliest ignorance on these may light,
Which when it sounds at best but echoes right;
Or blind affection, which doth ne'er advance

The truth, but gropes, and urges all by chance;
Or crafty malice might pretend this praise,
And think to ruin where it seemed to raise.
These are as some infamous bawd or whore
Should praise a matron. What could hurt her more?
But thou art proof against them, and indeed
Above th' ill fortune of them, or the need.
I therefore will begin: Soul of the Age!
The applause, delight, the wonder of our stage!
My Shakespeare, rise; I will not lodge thee by
Chaucer, or Spenser, or bid Beaumont lie
A little further, to make thee a room:
Thou art a monument without a tomb,
And art alive still, while thy book doth live,
And we have wits to read, and praise to give.
That I not mix thee so, my brain excuses,
I mean with great but disproportioned Muses,
For if I thought my judgement were of years,
I should commit thee surely with thy peers,
And tell how far thou didst our Lyly outshine,
Or sporting Kyd, or Marlowe's mighty line.
And though thou hadst small Latin and less Greek,
From thence to honour thee I would not seek
For names; but call forth thundering Aeschylus,
Euripides, and Sophocles to us,
Pacuvius, Accius, him of Cordova dead,
To live again, to hear thy buskin tread,
And shake a stage; or, when thy socks were on,
Leave thee alone for the comparison
Of all that insolent Greece or haughty Rome
Sent forth, or since did from their ashes come.
Triumph, my Britain, thou hast one to show
To whom all scenes of Europe homage owe.
He was not of an age, but for all time!
And all the Muses still were in their prime
When, like Apollo, he came forth to warm
Our ears, or, like a Mercury, to charm!
Nature herself was proud of his designs,
And joyed to wear the dressing of his lines!
Which were so richly spun, and woven so fit,
As, since, she will vouchsafe no other wit.
The merry Greek, tart Aristophanes,
Neat Terence, witty Plautus, now not please;
But antiquated and deserted lie,
As they were not of Nature's family.
Yet must I not give Nature all; thy art,
My gentle Shakespeare, must enjoy a part.
For though the poet's matter nature be,
His art doth give the fashion; and that he
Who casts to write a living line must sweat
(Such as thine are) and strike the second heat

Upon the Muses' anvil; turn the same,
And himself with it, that he thinks to frame,
Or for the laurel he may gain a scorn;
For a good poet's made as well as born.
And such wert thou. Look how the father's face
Lives in his issue, even so the race
Of Shakespeare's mind and manners brightly shines
In his well turned and true-filed lines:
In each of which he seems to shake a lance,
As brandished at the eyes of ignorance.
Sweet swan of Avon! what a sight it were
To see thee in our waters yet appear,
And make those flights upon the banks of Thames,
That did so take Eliza and our James!
But stay, I see thee in the hemisphere
Advanced, and made a constellation there:
Shine forth, thou Star of Poets, and with rage,
Or influence, chide or cheer the drooping stage,
Which, since thy flight from hence, hath mourned like night,
And despairs day, but for thy volume's light.

Shakespeare by Matthew Arnold

Others abide our question. Thou art free.
We ask and ask—Thou smilest and art still,
Out-topping knowledge. For the loftiest hill,
Who to the stars uncrowns his majesty,

Planting his steadfast footsteps in the sea,
Making the heaven of heavens his dwelling-place,
Spares but the cloudy border of his base
To the foil'd searching of mortality;

And thou, who didst the stars and sunbeams know,
Self-school'd, self-scann'd, self-honour'd, self-secure,
Didst tread on earth unguess'd at.—Better so!

All pains the immortal spirit must endure,
All weakness which impairs, all griefs which bow,
Find their sole speech in that victorious brow

An Epitaph On The Admirable Dramatic Poet W. Shakespeare by John Milton

What needs my Shakespeare for his honored bones
The labor of an age in piled stones?
Or that his hallowed reliques should be hid
Under a star-ypointing pyramid?

Dear son of Memory, great heir of Fame,
What need'st thou such weak witness of thy name?
Thou in our wonder and astonishment
Hast built thy self a livelong monument.
For whilst, to th' shame of slow-endeavoring art,
Thy easy numbers flow, and that each heart
Hath from the leaves of thy unvalued book
Those Delphic lines with deep impression took,
Then thou, our fancy of itself bereaving,
Dost make us marble with too much conceiving,
And so sepulchred in such pomp dost lie
That kings for such a tomb would wish to die.

Shakespeare by Henry Wadsworth Longfellow

A vision as of crowded city streets,
With human life in endless overflow;
Thunder of thoroughfares; trumpets that blow
To battle; clamor, in obscure retreats,
Of sailors landed from their anchored fleets;
Tolling of bells in turrets, and below
Voices of children, and bright flowers that throw
O'er garden-walls their intermingled sweets!
This vision comes to me when I unfold
The volume of the Poet paramount,
Whom all the Muses loved, not one alone;—
Into his hands they put the lyre of gold,
And, crowned with sacred laurel at their fount,
Placed him as Musagetes on their throne.

Elegy On Mr. William Shakespeare by William Basse

Renowned Spenser, lie a thought more nigh
To learned Chaucer, and rare Beaumont lie
A little nearer Spenser, to make room
For Shakespeare in your threefold, fourfold tomb.
To lodge all four in one bed, make a shift
Until Doomsday, for hardly will a fift
Betwixt this day and that by Fate be slain,
For whom your curtains may be drawn again.
If your precedency in death doth bar
A fourth place in your sacred sepulchre,
Under this carved marble of thine own,
Sleep, rare tragedian, Shakespeare, sleep alone;
Thy unmolested peace, unshared cave
Possess as lord, not tenant of thy grave,
That unto us and others it may be

Honour hereafter to be laid by thee.

Shakespeare by Vachel Lindsay

Would that in body and spirit Shakespeare came
Visible emperor of the deeds of Time,
With Justice still the genius of his rhyme,
Giving each man his due, each passion grace,
Impartial as the rain from Heaven's face
Or sunshine from the heaven-enthroned sun.
Sweet Swan of Avon, come to us again.
Teach us to write, and writing, to be men.

The Spirit of Shakespeare by George Meredith

Thy greatest knew thee, Mother Earth; unsoured
He knew thy sons. He probed from hell to hell
Of human passions, but of love deflowered
His wisdom was not, for he knew thee well.
Thence came the honeyed corner at his lips,
The conquering smile wherein his spirit sails
Calm as the God who the white sea-wave whips,
Yet full of speech and intershifting tales,
Close mirrors of us: thence had he the laugh
We feel is thine: broad as ten thousand beeves
At pasture! thence thy songs, that winnow chaff
From grain, bid sick Philosophy's last leaves
Whirl, if they have no response-they enforced
To fatten Earth when from her soul divorced.

To Shakespeare by Lord Alfred Douglas

Most tuneful singer, lover tenderest,
Most sad, most piteous, and most musical,
Thine is the shrine more pilgrim-worn than all
The shrines of singers; high above the rest
Thy trumpet sounds most loud, most manifest.
Yet better were it if a lonely call
Of woodland birds, a song, a madrigal,
Were all the jetsam of thy sea's unrest.

For now thy praises have become too loud
On vulgar lips, and every yelping cur
Yaps thee a paean; the whiles little men,
Not tall enough to worship in a crowd,

Spit their small wits at thee. Ah! better then
The broken shrine, the lonely worshipper.

To Shakespeare (I) by Frances Anne Kemble

If from the height of that celestial sphere
Where now thou dwell'st, spirit powerful and sweet!
Thou yet canst love the race that sojourn here,
How must thou joy, with pleasure not unmeet
For thy exalted state, to know how dear
Thy memory is held throughout the earth,
Beyond the favoured land that gave thee birth.
E'en in thy seat in Heaven, thou may'st receive
Thanks, praise, and love, and wonder ever new,
From human hearts, who in thy verse perceive
All that humanity calls good and true;
Nor dost thou for each mortal blemish grieve,
They from thy glorious works have fall'n away,
As from thy soul its outward form of clay.

To Shakespeare (II) by Frances Anne Kemble

Oft, when my lips I open to rehearse
Thy wondrous spells of wisdom and of power,
And that my voice and thy immortal verse
On listening ears and hearts I mingled pour,
I shrink dismayed—and awful doth appear
The vain presumption of my own weak deed;
Thy glorious spirit seems to mine so near,
That suddenly I tremble as I read—
Thee an invisible auditor I fear:
Oh, if it might be so, my master dear!
With what beseeching would I pray to thee,
To make me equal to my noble task,
Succour from thee, how humbly would I ask,
Thy worthiest works to utter worthily.

To Shakespeare (III) by Frances Anne Kemble

Shelter and succour such as common men
Afford the weaker partners of their fate,
Have I derived from thee—from thee, most great
And powerful genius! whose sublime control,
Still from thy grave governs each human soul,
That reads the wondrous records of thy pen.

From sordid sorrows thou hast set me free,
And turned from want's grim ways my tottering feet,
And to sad empty hours, given royally,
A labour, than all leisure far more sweet:
The daily bread, for which we humbly pray,
Thou gavest me as if I were thy child,
And still with converse noble, wise, and mild,
Charmed from despair my sinking soul away;
Shall I not bless the need, to which was given
Of all the angels in the host of heaven,
Thee, for my guardian, spirit strong and bland!
Lord of the speech of my dear native land!

Shakespeare and Milton by Walter Savage Landor

The tongue of England, that which myriads
Have spoken and will speak, were paralyz'd
Hereafter, but two mighty men stand forth
Above the flight of ages, two alone;
One crying out,
All nations spoke through me.
The other:
True; and through this trumpet burst God's word;
The fall of Angels, and the doom
First of immortal, then of mortal, Man.
Glory! be glory! not to me, to God.

A Shakespeare Memorial by Alfred Austin

Why should we lodge in marble or in bronze
Spirits more vast than earth, or sea, or sky?
Wiser the silent worshipper that cons
Their words for wisdom that will never die.
Unto the favourite of the passing hour
Erect the statue and parade the bust;
Whereon decisive Time will slowly shower
Oblivion's refuse and disdainful dust.
The Monarchs of the Mind, self-sceptred Kings,
Need no memento to transmit their name:
Throned on their thoughts and high imaginings,
They are the Lords, not sycophants of Fame.
Raise pedestals to perishable stuff:
Gods for themselves are monuments enough.

Shakespeare by Mathilde Blind

Yearning to know herself for all she was,
Her passionate clash of warring good and ill,
Her new life ever ground in Death's old mill,
With every delicate detail and en masse,—
Blind Nature strove. Lo, then it came to pass,
That Time, to work out her unconscious Will,
Once wrought the Mind which she had groped for still,
And she beheld herself as in a glass.

The world of men, unrolled before our sight,
Showed like a map, where stream and waterfall
And village-cradling vale and cloud-capped height
Stand faithfully recorded, great and small;
For Shakespeare was, and at his touch, with light
Impartial as the Sun's, revealed the All.

Shakespeare by Robert Crawford

And what think ye of Shakespeare? 'Twas not he
Of Stratford is the lord of England's lyre;
Ay, not the rustic lad, whoe'er it be,
Momentous in his doing and desire.
But little Latin and less Greek? Ah, no!
It was a teeming scholar who enwrought
The wondrous pages where the wisest go
For th' culmination of the life of thought.
No jovial actor, no mere Shakescene who
Found it so hard his dear name to indite,
The marvellous pictures of our nature drew
And limned the universe in his delight.
We do not know the man; but 'twas not Will
Whose hand is on the lyre of England still.

Shakespeare by Thomas Gent

While o'er this pageant of sublunar things
Oblivion spreads her unrelenting wings,
And sweeps adown her dark unebbing tide
Man, and his mightiest monuments of pride-
Alone, aloft, immutable, sublime,
Star-like, ensphered above the track of time,
Great SHAKSPEARE beams with undiminish'd ray.
His bright creations sacred from decay,
Like Nature's self, whose living form he drew,
Though still the same, still beautiful and new.

He came, untaught in academic bowers,
A gift to Glory from the Sylvan powers:
But what keen Sage, with all the science fraught,
By elder bards or later critics taught,
Shall count the cords of his mellifluous shell,
Span the vast fabric of his fame, and tell
By what strange arts he bade the structure rise-
On what deep site the strong foundation lies?
This, why should scholiasts labour to reveal?
We all can answer it, we all can feel,
Ten thousand sympathies, attesting, start-
For SHAKSPEARE'S Temple, is the human heart!

Lord of a throne which mortal ne'er shall share-
Despot adored! he rales and revels there.
Who but has found, where'er his track hath been,
Through life's oft shifting, multifarious scene,
Still at his side the genial Bard attend,
His loved companion, counsellor, and friend!

The Thespian Sisters nurtured in the schools
Of Greece and Rome, and long coerced by rules,
Scarce moved the inmates of their native hearth
With tiny pathos and with trivial mirth,
Till She, great muse of daring enterprise,
Delighted ENGLAND! saw her SHAKSPEARE rise!

Then, first aroused in that appointed hour,
The Tragic Muse confess'd th' inspiring power;
Sudden before the startled earth she stood,
A giant spectre, weeping tears and blood;
Guilt shrunk appall'd, Despair embraced his shroud,
And Terror shriek'd, and Pity sobb'd aloud;-
Then, first Thalia with dilated ken
And quicken'd footstep pierced the walks of men;
Then Folly blush'd, Vice fled the general hiss,
Delight met Reason with a loving kiss;
At Satire's glance Pride smooth'd his low'ring crest,
The Graces weaved the dance.-And last and best
Came Momus down in Falstaff's form to earth.
To make the world one universe of mirth!

Such Sympathies the glorious Bard endear!
Thus fair he walks in Man's diurnal sphere.
But when, upborne on bright Invention's wings.
He dares the realms of uncreated things,
Forms more divine, more dreadful, start to view,
Than ever Hades or Olympus knew.
Round the dark cauldron, terrible and fell,
The midnight Witches breathe the songs of hell;
Delighted Ariel wings his fiery way

To whirl the storm, the wheeling Orbs to stay;
Then bathes in honey-dews, and sleeps in flowers;
Meanwhile, young Oberon, girt with shadowy powers,
Pursues o'er Ocean's verge the pale cold Moon,
Or hymns her, riding in her highest noon.

Thus graced, thus glorified, shall SHAKSPEARE crave
The Sculptor's skill, the pageant of the grave?
HE needs it not-but Gratitude demands
This votive offering at his Country's hands.
Haply, e'er now, from blissful bowers on high,
From some Parnassus of the empyreal sky,
Pleased, o'er this dome the gentle Spirit bends,
Accepts the gift, and hails us as his friends-
Yet smiles, perchance, to think when envious Time
O'er Bust and Urn shall bid his ivies climb,
When Palaces and Pyramids shall fall-
HIS PAGE SHALL TRIUMPH-still surviving all-
'Till Earth itself, 'like breath upon the wind,'
Shall melt away, 'nor leave a rack behind!'

Shakespeare's Mourners by John Bannister Tabb

I saw the grave of Shakespeare in a dream,
And round about it grouped a wondrous throng,
His own majestic mourners, who belong
Forever to the Stage of Life, and seem
The rivals of reality. Supreme
Stood Hamlet, as erewhile the graves among,
Mantled in thought: and sad Ophelia sung
The same swan-dirge she chanted in the stream.
Othello, dark in destiny's eclipse,
Laid on the tomb a lily. Near him wept
Dejected Constance. Fair Cordelia's lips
Moved prayerfully the while her father slept,
And each and all, inspired of vital breath,
Kept vigil o'er the sacred spoils of death.

Shakespeare by Philip Henry Savage

Through time untimed, if truly great, a Name
Reverence compels and, that forgotten, shame.
But in the stress of living you shall scan,
Yea, touch and censure, great or small, the Man.

Shakespeare by Lucretia Maria Davidson

Shakspeare!' with all thy faults, (and few have more,)
I love thee still,' and still will con thee o'er.
Heaven, in compassion to man's erring heart,
Gave thee of virtue — then, of vice a part,
Lest we, in wonder here, should bow before thee,
Break God's commandment, worship, and adore thee:
But admiration now, and sorrow join;
His works we reverence, while we pity thine.

Shakespeare by Frederick George Scott

Unseen in the great minister dome of time,
Whose shafts are centuries, its spangled roof
The vaulted universe, our master sits,
And organ-voices like a far-off chime
Roll thro' the aisles of thought. The sunlight flits

From arch to arch, and, as he sits aloof,
Kings, heroes, priests, in concourse vast, sublime,
Glances of love and cries from battle-field,
His wizard power breathes on the living air.
Warm faces gleam and pass, child, woman, man,

In the long multitude; but he, concealed,
Our bard eludes us, vainly each face we scan,
It is not he; his features are not there;
But, being thus hid, his greatness is revealed.

Shakespeare's Kingdom by Alfred Noyes

When Shakespeare came to London
He met no shouting throngs;
He carried in his knapsack
A scroll of quiet songs.

No proud heraldic trumpet
Acclaimed him on his way;
Their court and camp have perished;
The songs live on for ay.

Nobody saw or heard them,
But, all around him there,
Spirits of light and music
Went treading the April air.

He passed like any pedlar,
Yet he had wealth untold.
The galleons of th' armada
Could not contain his gold.

The kings rode on to darkness.
In England's conquering hour,
Unseen arrived her splendour;
Unknown, her conquering power.

Shakespeare 1916 by Sir Ronald Ross

Now when the sinking Sun reeketh with blood,
And the gore-gushing vapors rent by him
Rend him and bury him: now the World is dim
As when great thunders gather for the flood,
And in the darkness men die where they stood,
And dying slay, or scatter'd limb from limb
Cease in a flash where mad-eyed cherubim
Of Death destroy them in the night and mud:
When landmarks vanish—murder is become
A glory—cowardice, conscience— and to lie,
A law—to govern, but to serve a time:—
We dying, lifting bloodied eyes and dumb,
Behold the silver star serene on high,
That is thy spirit there, O Master Mind sublime.

Song, In Imitation of Shakspeare's by James Beattie

I
Blow, blow, thou vernal gale!
Thy balm will not avail
To ease my aching breast;
Though thou the billows smooth,
Thy murmurs cannot soothe
My weary soul to rest.

II
Flow, flow, thou tuneful stream!
Infuse the easy dream
Into the peaceful soul;
But thou canst not compose
The tumult of my woes,
Though soft thy waters roll.

III
Blush, blush, ye fairest flowers!

Beauties surpassing yours
My Rosalind adorn;
Nor is the Winter's blast,
That lays your glories waste,
So killing as her scorn.

IV
Breathe, breathe, ye tender lays,
That linger down the maze
Of yonder winding grove;
O let your soft control
Bend her relenting soul
To pity and to love.

V
Fade, fade, ye flowerets fair!
Gales, fan no more the air!
Ye streams, forget to glide;
Be hush'd each vernal strain;
Since nought can soothe my pain,
Nor mitigate her pride.

In A Letter To C. P. Esq. In Imitation Of Shakspeare by William Cowper

Trust me the meed of praise, dealt thriftily
From the nice scale of judgement, honours more
Than does the lavish and o'erbearing tide
Of profuse courtesy. Not all the gems
Of India's richest soil at random spread
O'er the gay vesture of some glittering dame,
Give such alluring vantage to the person,
As the scant lustre of a few, with choice
And comely guise of ornament disposed.

Shakspeare. (An Ode For His Three-Hundredth Birthday) by Martin Farquhar Tupper

I.
Immortal! risen to thy Rest,
Immortal! throned among the Blest,
Immortal! long an heir sublime
Of realms outreaching space and time,—
How shall we dare, or hope, to raise
A fitting homage of high praise
To please thy Spirit, sphered on high
Where planets roll and comets fly?
How may not thy pure fame be marr'd
By the damp breath of earthly bard,

Presuming in his zeal too bold
To gild the bright refinèd gold?
Or how canst thou, fill'd with God's love,
And tranced among the saints above,
Endure that men should seem and be
Idolaters in praise of thee!
Forgive our love, forgive our zeal,—
We cannot guess how spirits feel;
And may our homage offered thus
Please HIM who made both thee, and us!

II.
Immortal also on this darker Earth
As in those brighter spheres,
Now will we consecrate our Shakespeare's birth,
This day three hundred years!
And so from age to age for evermore
His glory shall extend,
With men of every land the wide world o'er,
Till Time itself shall end!
For, he is our's; and well with pride and joy
England may bless her son,
The Stratford scholar and the Warwick boy
That every crown hath won!
Let others boast their wisest and their best,
To each a prize may fall;
Genius gives one apiece to all the rest,
But Shakspeare claims them all!

III.
A Homer, in majestic eloquence,
A Terence, for keen wit and stinging sense,
Brighter than Pindar in his loftiest flight,
Darker than Æschylus for deeds of night,
An Ovid, in the story-pictured page,
A Juvenal, to lash the vicious age,
Graceful as Horace and more skill'd to please,
Tender as pity-stirring Sophocles,
Free as Anacreon, as Martial neat,
Than Virgil's self more delicately sweet,—
O let those ancients bend before Thee now,
And pile their many chaplets on one brow!—
Milton was great, and of divinest song,
Spenser melodious, Chaucer rough and strong,—
The vigorous Dryden, and the classic Gray,
And awful Danté, soaring far away,
Schiller and Göethe, stirring up the strife,
And Molière, dropping laughter into life,
Burns, a full spring of nature, Hood of wit,
And Tennyson, most rare and exquisite,
To each and all belongs the laurell'd crown,

And woe to him who drags their honours down,—
Yet, Shakspeare, thou wert all these lights combined,
O manysided crystal of mankind!

IV.
The jealous Moor, the thoughtful Dane,
The witty rare fat knight,
And grand old Lear half-insane,
And fell Iago's spite,
And Romeo's love, and Tybalt's hate,
And Bolinbroke in regal state,
And he that murdered sleep,—
And ruthless Shylock's bloody bond,
And Prosper with his broken wand
Long buried fathoms deep!
Frank Juliet too,— and that soft pair
Helen and Hermia, lilies fair
As growing on one stem,
Love-crazed Ophelia, drown'd ah! drown'd,
And wanton Cleopatra, crown'd
With Egypt's diadem;
The young Miranda most admired,
Cordelia's filial heart,
Sly Beatrice with wit inspired,
And Ariel's tricksey part,
Fair Rosalind,— sweet banishèd,
And gentle Desdemona — dead!—
Ay these, all these, and crowds beside,
Heroes, jesters, courtiers, clowns,
Girls in grief, or kings in pride,
Threats and crimes, and jokes, and frowns,
Witches, fairies, ghosts, and elves,
All our fancies, all ourselves,—
O! thou hast pictured with thy pen
All phases of all hearts of men,
And in thy various page survives
The Panorama of our lives!

V.
O Paragon unthought before,
O miracle of selftaught lore,
A universe of wit and worth,
The admirable Man of earth,
There is nor thing, nor thought, nor whim,
Untouch'd and unadorn'd by him;
No theme unsung, no truth untold
Of Earth's museum, new or old:
All Nature's hidden things he saw,
Intuitive to every law;
Glancing with supernal scan
At all the knowledge spelt by man;

While, for each rule and craft of Art
He grasp'd it amply, whole and part:
Like travel-wise Ulysses well he knew
Peoples and cities, men and manners too;
With shrewd but ever charitable ken
He read, and wrote out fair, the hearts of men;
Yet, in self-knowledge vers'd, a sage outright,
His giant soul was humble in its might!
O gentle, happy, modest mind,
O genial, cheerful, frank and kind,
Not even could domestic strife
Sour the sweetness of thy life,—
But wheresoe'er thy foot might roam,
Divorced from that Xantipp'd home,
Friends ever found thee,— ay, and foes,
Cordial to these, and kind to those;
Brave, loving, patient, generous, just, and good,—
Beloved by all, our matchless Shakspeare stood!

VI.

Where are thy glorious works unknown?
Who hath not heard thy fame?
On every shore, in every zone,
The World, with glad acclaim,
Yea, from the cottage to the throne,
Hath magnified thy name!
From far Australia to Vancouver's pines,
From the High Alps to Russia's deepest mines,
From China, with her English lesson learnt,
To Chili, wailing for her daughters burnt;
There, everywhere, our Shakspeare breathes and moves
In the sweet ether of all human loves!—
Where rent America now writhes in woe,
Where Nile and Danube, Thames and Ganges flow,
Wherever England sails, and human kind
Anywhere feels in heart, and thinks in mind,
There, everywhere, our Shakspeare's voice is heard,
By him all souls are thrill'd, and cheer'd, and stirr'd;
Each passion flows or ebbs, as Shakspeare speaks,
Hate knits the brow, or terror pales the cheeks,
Love lights the eyes, or pity melts the heart,
And all men bow beneath our Poet's art!

VII.

What monument to rear,
What worthy offering?—
Nought lacks thy glory here
Of all thy sons can bring:
Long since, a twin-sphered brother spake,
How vain it were to raise
To such a Name, for Memory's sake,

Its pyramid of praise:
Our Shakspeare needs no sculptured stones,
No temple for his honoured bones!
But haply in his native street
Beside the rescued home
Hallowed by his infant feet
Whereto all pilgrims roam,
A College well might rear its head,
That Townsman's name to bear,
And brother-actors' sons he bred
To light and learning there!
And, for great London and its throngs,—
To Shakspeare of old right belongs
The Shakspeare Bridge, with Shakspeare scenes
Sculptured upon its pannell'd screens,
Colossus-like the Thames to span,
And telling every passing man
Where a poor player in his youth
Served Heaven and Earth by mimic truth,
And wrapped in Art's and Nature's robe,
Leased,— 'twas his Heritage, — the Globe!—

VIII.
Great Magician for all time,
Denizen of every clime,
Darling poet of mankind,
Master of the human mind,
Nature's very priest and king,—
Take the gifts thy children bring!
Let thy Spirit, hovering o'er
Thine earthly home and haunts of yore,
In its wisdom, wealth, and worth,
Shine upon us from above,
While thy kinsmen here on earth
Thus with pious care and love
Celebrate our Shakspeare's birth.

On The Site of A Mulberry-Tree; Planted By Wm. Shakspeare; Felled By The Rev. F. Gastrell by Dante Gabriel Rossetti

This tree, here fall'n, no common birth or death
Shared with its kind. The world's enfranchised son,
Who found the trees of Life and Knowledge one,
Here set it, frailer than his laurel-wreath.
Shall not the wretch whose hand it fell beneath
Rank also singly—the supreme unhung?
Lo! Sheppard, Turpin, pleading with black tongue
This viler thief's unsuffocated breath!
We'll search thy glossary, Shakspeare! whence almost,

And whence alone, some name shall be reveal'd
For this deaf drudge, to whom no length of ears
Sufficed to catch the music of the spheres;
Whose soul is carrion now,—too mean to yield
Some Starveling's ninth allotment of a ghost.

www.ingramcontent.com/pod-product-compliance
Lightning Source LLC
Chambersburg PA
CBHW071505040426
42444CB00008B/1510